Thinking Th

Genera
Graham Slater and C. S. Rodd

8. Salvation

Thinking Things Through

Already Published

In Preparation

Thinking Things Through

8. Salvation

T. J. Gorringe

EPWORTH PRESS

ISBN 0-7162-0540-8

First published 2000
by Epworth Press
20 Ivatt Way,
Peterborough
PE3 7PG

Typeset by C. S. Rodd
Printed and bound by
Biddles Ltd
Guildford and King's Lynn

Contents

General Introduction

The great Swiss theologian, Hans Küng, has said that his aim in all his writings is to enable his readers to hold their faith with confidence and not with a bad conscience. This new series, prompted by the conviction that Christians need to think through their faith but often lack appropriate help in so doing, has a similar aim. Moreover, the assistance that it seeks to offer is related to another conviction: that many church members need persuading that theologians are concerned in any way with their problems and that theology can be at all relevant to their lives.

In such a situation, it is essential, we are sure, to begin with life and with church life. Only in that way can we be confident that we are dealing with grassroots issues. Plainly, however, it is not enough to identify the questions where they arise; we must also indicate the sources of help – if not of all the answers – in as non-technical a way as possible.

In some volumes, these tasks will be tackled in sequence; in others, they will be interwoven. Whatever the precise format, however, our hope is that, through this interaction, difficulties will be faced, fears dispelled, open discussion promoted, and faith informed and strengthened.

The books can either be read by individuals on their own or used in groups. We hope the questions at the end of each chapter will be useful both as a check that the text has been understood and as a spur to reflection and discussion.

Later volumes will deal with the existence of God, Jesus, the Holy Spirit, creation and providence, and prayer.

GRAHAM SLATER AND C. S. RODD

Preface

I am very grateful to Graham Slater, C. S. Rodd, and Epworth Press for inviting an Anabaptist Anglican with deep roots in eucharistic practice to write this little book. I am grateful for the comments of the Editorial Board, to which I have tried to respond, and especially to Magdalen Gorringe, who wanted a much more radical overhaul than I was able to provide. Her feminist version would doubtless have been more interesting and more challenging, but we will have to wait for it.

TIM GORRINGE

Part 1

Questions About Salvation

1

A Prison Visit

Rebecca was apprehensive. She'd met Tom just a fortnight before, on the train coming down from Scotland, and they'd got on wonderfully. They'd been out once since, but now for their second 'date' he was taking her to the local prison, for an evening discussion group! She'd known of the prison for years, going past it in the bus on the way to school as a child, but had never given it much thought. The prospect of going inside rather frightened her.

And then, though she found Tom attractive, intelligent and fun he had one big drawback: he wasn't a Christian. For nearly three years now, since she moved back to her home town after university, where she had studied music, St Michael's had been at the heart of her social life as well as immeasurably strengthening her faith. It was a dynamic, lively church, with an overwhelmingly young congregation. It buoyed her up to go there. It was the sort of church which might have been expected to do something with the prison, but it was quite a way on the other side of town, at the heart of a rather well-to-do suburb, and in any case there were so many weekday activities going on there was hardly room for another. Rebecca was involved in the youth outreach scheme, but this didn't have a lot of contact with the kids from 'downtown'. St Michael's tended to concentrate on its own very sizeable clientele, which drew people together from all over the city, but very few, if any, from the downtown areas.

She shared her apprehensions about the visit when Tom came to pick her up, but he told her there wouldn't be a problem. Her heart sank, though, as they stood outside the reinforced steel door, waiting for a prison officer to open up for them. Four or five others joined them in the courtyard just inside the main gate, and then the chaplain, Fr David, came down to take them up to the chapel, where the discussions were held. She found the clang of iron doors, the opening and shutting of locks every few yards, the institutional smell, the prison officers standing about at key points, the prisoners filing by in small groups, both intimidating and depressing. Very shortly, however, they were ushered in to the chapel, rather 'high' for her taste, but still something with which she could identify. After five minutes or so a dozen prisoners joined them in a discussion circle, and two prison officers took their seats near the door.

Apart from being a prison visitor in his spare time, Tom taught drama at the local College of Further Education, and Fr David had asked him to lead a discussion. He had wanted to do role play, but the governor had said 'No', so he chose instead to use some video clips from *Dead Man Walking*, a film based on the true story of a Catholic nun, Helen Prejean, who had attempted to get a young black prisoner, sentenced to death, to face up to his guilt, and to mediate between him and the families of his victims. Being opposed to the death penalty she tried, unsuccessfully, to get his sentence commuted.

After showing the clips, Tom began the discussion. 'I don't want to focus too much on the death penalty. Fortunately that's not our problem over here. The film raises lots of other issues, and I'd like to see how you identify them.'

Stuart, a black prisoner, was the first to speak. 'In the bits you showed us,' he said, 'it was all about him facing up to his guilt. He said he didn't do it, but he did. The nun says he has to acknowledge that to be forgiven.'

'And what do you think about that?'

'She's right. There's lots of blokes in here who say they're not guilty, but they are. I think forgiveness is important. It helps you start again. It gives you a clean slate.' 'I don't agree with that,' said Dave, another prisoner. 'Not everyone in here is guilty. Some of us got in here by mistake, or because we were set up, or because we were unlucky. And none of us did what that bloke did.'

Tom asked: 'But do you think forgiveness is important?'

4

'No, not really. Life's treated me pretty rough. I expect it had treated that black kid pretty rough. He ended up in the electric chair. What's forgiveness got to do with it?'

Fr David intervened. 'But look. Suppose you do do something wrong. Suppose you harm someone, or kill someone, don't you need to ask for forgiveness?'

'I think you do,' said Stuart, 'because being guilty destroys you. It eats you up. It makes you angry, and you just behave worse and worse.'

'Why do you think that is?'

'I don't know. Maybe you hate yourself for what you've done.'

'Exactly,' Fr David agreed. 'Self-hatred is the problem. We always think self-love is the problem, but it isn't. It's self-hatred. If we can't love ourselves, we can't love others either.'

'The problem is,' said Stuart, 'getting the forgiveness. You can't forgive yourself. Only the people you hurt can forgive. Like the parents in the film. One lot would forgive, and the others wouldn't.'

'In chapel on Sunday mornings,' said another prisoner, Steve, 'we make confession, and you pronounce forgiveness.'

'But that's a problem,' said Stuart. 'How can God forgive? He's not the one we've hurt. God's not the victim.'

'Ah, but isn't he?' asked Fr David.

'Well, how is he?'

'Think about it,' Fr David replied. 'Christ was executed, just like that young black prisoner. He died as a criminal.'

'Yes, but he was innocent,' said Stuart. 'Like Dave says, not everyone in prison is guilty.'

'That's precisely the point. Because he was a victim, he's in a position to forgive offenders. And Christ gave the power of forgiving sins to the church. That's why we hear confession and pronounce forgiveness.'

'I agree with Stuart,' said Tom. 'All that seems very remote from everyday life to me. What Sister Helen was concerned

5

about was healing the hurt of those parents and trying to get the system to behave more humanely. The problem with that system is that it's an eye for an eye, and it gets you nowhere.'

'OK, but how do you heal the hurt of the parents?' asked Fr David.

'You can't,' said Stuart. 'You can't bring the kids they lost back.'

'That's true, but I think you can make the hurt less bitter. And just as guilt can destroy you, so can hate. They're the same thing really – two sides of the same coin.'

'But forgiveness is ambiguous as well, isn't it?' said Tom. 'There's another play – well, a musical called *Les Misérables* – which we could look at another time. It's about someone who's imprisoned in the galleys, escapes, and is then hunted for years by a policeman. Finally, he has the policeman in his power, but he lets him go. And the policeman can't bear the forgiveness, and commits suicide.'

'So what are you saying?'

'Well, in that case, forgiveness destroyed him, didn't it. He couldn't live with himself.'

'But there we come back to self-hatred,' Fr David interposed. 'His problem was pride. If he'd acknowledged he was at fault, and accepted that he'd been wrong, and needed forgiveness, he would have been saved.'

'Saved?'

'Well, made whole – able to lead a useful life instead of being consumed by this passion of hatred, which really wasted his life.'

'Inner demons,' said Tom.

'Exactly.'

'But you can't get away from inner demons,' said Stuart. 'We've all got them.' 'Yes, they're our shadow. We repress all the bad things we want to do, and they grow inside us and sometimes come to control us.'

'And how are you supposed to deal with that?'

'By learning to forgive yourself,' Fr David countered at once. 'By facing your shadow. It may seem strange, but that's what we do every Sunday morning in chapel. That's what confession of sins is all about.'

'So for you,' said Tom, 'going to church is really about – learning to be human.'

'You're learning!'

'H'm, I'm not sure I can go along with that.'

Tom and Rebecca went for a drink afterwards. Rebecca had to agree that it hadn't been nearly as bad as she thought it would be. She was astonished at how articulate the prisoners had been.

'But what did you expect?' asked Tom.

'I don't know. I don't know what I expected. Well, I suppose I thought they might be obviously evil and vicious men, but they weren't. They were ordinary.'

'There but for the grace of God go I!'

'Exactly ... But I thought you didn't believe in God's grace.'

'I don't. It's just a manner of speaking.'

'The chaplain seemed a good person.'

'He's a very good person. He respects the men and he doesn't push religion down their throats.'

Rebecca was quiet. After a while she said, 'It's not a question of pushing religion down people's throats. It's a question of sharing the gospel.'

'Which is?'

'Which is what Fr David said. Forgiveness.'

'But I agree with Stuart. There's a problem with God forgiving us. It seems too easy to me.'

'Tom,' said Rebecca, 'will you do something for me? I've come to your discussion group, and I've really enjoyed it. But will you come to one of mine? We have a discussion group every Wednesday evening, which our curate runs.

He's really good. It would be good to discuss these questions
there.'

'Do I have to?'

'No, you don't have to. I'd like you to.'

'You blackmailer. I guess I'll have to then . . .'

Questions for discussion

1. To what extent is guilt something we need to be saved from,
and to what extent is it something we can't be human without?

2. Is it only the victim who can forgive, as Stuart thinks, or can
the church make God's forgiveness available, as Fr David
argues?

3. In telling the story from *Les Misérables*, Tom argues that
forgiveness can be ambiguous. Is that right, or is it always a
straightforward good?

2

The Emmaus Course

The Emmaus course which St Michael's ran was ostensibly for enquirers, but in point of fact very few enquirers ever came. Tom's visit was therefore something of a rarity, and Rebecca had spoken to Adrian, the curate who ran the course, about him coming. He could see that the visit was important to her, but didn't ask why; and he was pleased with the challenge, and the confidence she had in him. The discussion obviously had to centre on the heart of the faith: on Christ's death for sinners, the atonement.

For his part, it was now Tom's turn to feel apprehensive. 'An agnostic Daniel in a den of Christians!' as he put it when he met Rebecca to go to the meeting. This was held in a large, bright, modern room and a dozen people turned up in addition to Adrian. As far as he could tell, Tom was the only non-Christian.

'As you'll remember,' said Adrian, 'this week we're due to discuss the atonement. That's a word which was made up at the beginning of the sixteenth century and literally means 'at-one-ment'. It's our reflection on what Christ has done to make God and human beings at one, when our sin has created a gap between God and ourselves. I mentioned last week that I'd like one or two members of the group to talk about what it means to them. Is there anyone who's prepared to start us off?'

Dawn was the first to speak. 'Some of you know my story already,' she said, 'but not all of you. So those who do will have to forgive me.

'I was a drop out at school, and when I left I never had a proper job. Things weren't good at home, so I moved out, and I started going with a bloke who used drugs, and I got into the habit. We were squatting, and we had no money, so we had to make what we could by pilfering things and selling them. Then I got pregnant, and this bloke just didn't want to know.

He kicked me out of the squat, and I was on my own. I was with various other people for a while, but the drug habit was bad, and eventually someone persuaded me to have an abortion.

'After that I don't know what happened. I got terribly depressed, and finally I decided to end it all. I took a massive overdose, and next thing I knew I was in hospital. Well, that's where my luck finally changed. The sister on my ward is actually a member of this church. She listened to my story, and said that if I would go on a rehab programme I could come and live in her flat. I did. I went through the programme – that was really hard. But the sister – Marie, most of you know her – supported me, and then got me on some training courses. I did OK, and now I have a job, and I'm in a flat of my own.

'But the most important thing she did for me was to introduce me to Jesus. We used to pray together, and she would talk to me about her faith. And all of a sudden I got this wonderful feeling, and I knew that Jesus loved me, and that he died for me. I started attending church and I've been coming for, what, three years now? I think I started a bit earlier than you, Rebecca.'

Even though many of the group had heard the story before they were visibly moved.

'I know just what you mean,' said another of the group, Alan. 'I strayed from the straight and narrow as well, and then I found the Lord. And this is the most wonderful thing. If ever I'm a bit depressed, or find myself getting wound up or angry I just remember that Jesus died for me, and that fills me with sweetness. It's the incomparable love of God shown for sinners. I find it in that beautiful hymn we sing sometimes:

> Glory be to Jesus,
> Who, in bitter pains,
> Poured for me the life-blood
> From his sacred veins.

Grace and life eternal
In that blood I find;
Blest be his compassion,
Infinitely kind.

It was obvious that Alan spoke for the whole group, who were caught up in his emotion.

Adrian now turned to Tom. 'What do you make of all this, Tom?'

'I don't know,' said Tom. 'I recognize the truth of the experience. I don't question that, and I don't want to call into question anything Dawn or Alan have said – but I can't see where the death comes in. I could tell you stories from my experience at the prison of people who've come good, and started a new life, and God has had nothing to do with it.'

'You don't know that,' interjected Adrian.

'I don't know that, of course. But what I mean is, they didn't have any kind of conversion experience, or at least, not to God or Jesus. And the death imagery worries me. To be frank, it's one of the things I find least attractive about Christianity. It seems to me to imply a fascination with pain and suffering, a kind of sadomasochism. Why is the death so central?'

'You'll agree,' said Adrian, 'that all human beings are sinners.'

'Actually, "sin" isn't a category I use, but if you mean by that that nobody's perfect, then of course.'

'OK, and as you know from prison, all sin has to be punished because otherwise you'd have moral chaos and the barriers between good and evil would just dissolve. Well, humans have been sinning since the beginning of time, and all this sin creates a tremendous barrier between human beings and God. And that barrier means that human beings are cut off from the source of their life, their good. Without God the end for human beings is death, both here and now, and eternally. By death here and now I mean the kind of thing Dawn was talking about. Unless we

11

are oriented on God we get trapped into ways of life which destroy us and all around us. You must have seen many examples of that in the prison.'

Tom nodded.

'And so,' Adrian went on, 'God takes the situation into his own hands. He sends his Son to die for us. In doing that he judges the sin, and pays the penalty at the same time. Jesus is the Judge, but he takes our place in the dock and dies for us. Our sin meant that we were condemned to death. But since Jesus has died in our place there is no longer any condemnation. We are set free to live as new people. The word Paul uses for this comes from the law courts: it's "justification". We are "justified". That means, the Judge acquits us, pronounces us free and no longer guilty.'

'Sounds like a legal fiction to me,' said Tom.

'No, on the contrary. It's not a legal fiction. It's the most real thing in the world. It's changed the human situation for everyone.'

'But what about those people who don't know Christ, or who don't want to know him, like me?'

'It's your choice,' said Alan.

'Not for millions of Hindus or Muslims or Buddhists, today or through the ages. What do you think happens to them?'

'I don't know,' said Alan. 'It sounds hard, but I think they go to hell. There's no salvation except through Christ.'

'I wouldn't go that far,' said Adrian.' I don't think it's up to us to say. God will deal with them in his own wisdom and mercy. But in Christian cultures I think it's a different matter. For those of us who are Christians the onus is on us to preach the gospel, to give everyone a chance to hear. If we fail to do that, then we will be judged. But when we do do it, then people are free to say "No". The gospel is an offer. It's not compulsory. But if people choose against God, then they choose against their highest good. They choose death in place of life. That's the meaning of free will.'

12

'So you think,' said Tom, 'that those who choose against God are condemned to eternal death.'

'I do,' said Adrian.

'Hell fire and torments and all that?'

'No, I wouldn't say that, though there are plenty of passages in Scripture which talk about that. But no. In my understanding people can choose to reject God, who is the source of all life. And the corollary of that choice is the end of life – real death.'

'If you don't mind me saying so,' said Tom, 'that seems very simplistic to me. The choices we make are never free in an uncomplicated sense. On the contrary, our background, our education, our genes all determine them. For instance, suppose the worst prisoner in our jail had been swapped in his cradle with the Prince of Wales. Do you think he'd be in jail now? And what would the Prince of Wales be doing if he'd been brought up by a single Mum in the council estate on the other side of town?'

'I don't know,' said someone, 'but he'd being doing something with houses. Building them or pulling them down. If he'd made it he'd be an architect.'

General laughter followed this sally.

'That's all very well,' said Adrian, 'but no matter who you are you have to take responsibility for your actions. God will hold us all to account. This is part of the glory of what it is to be human, that God has given us free choice. To deny our responsibility is to deny our humanity.'

'Suppose you're fourteen,' said Tom, 'and you're in an area where drugs are everywhere. Some pusher gets you hooked on heroin or cocaine. What free choice do you have? That's an absurdly unreal view of what life is really like.'

'I don't think so at all. By fourteen you know right from wrong. The problem is the disintegration of family life.'

'One of the problems. Poverty and lack of opportunity are others. But you've just agreed with me. If you're born to caring

13

and able parents, you're lucky. What if you're born to feckless and stupid ones. What chance do you have?'

'That's the problem the church identifies as "original sin".'

'Sorry, you've lost me.'

'What we mean by "original sin" is that damaged people damage people. But we're all damaged. The damage goes right the way back to the start of time. That's why we need a Saviour. Only someone totally outside that pattern of damage can help us.'

'And how do you think that happens?'

'That's what Dawn and Alan have been talking about. God sends his Son to die for us. He wipes out the guilt we've accrued and enables us to start again.'

'That may happen for Dawn and Alan and a few people like them, but not for the majority of people.'

'But don't you see. That's why the work of evangelization is so important. We have to share with everyone the knowledge of God's forgiveness and love.'

'You don't seem very successful. Only seven per cent of the entire population of this country go to churches of any kind.'

'Far more believe, though.'

'But are they saved from original sin? From poor parenting, and child abuse, and social deprivation.'

'I didn't say they were identical with original sin.'

'Then I don't know what you're talking about.'

'I hope you didn't find that too awful,' said Rebecca as they walked home.

'No, but I'm not a convert. There are still too many unanswered questions, and I don't buy what Adrian said about what he called "justification".'

'You were a bit hard on him.'

'He can look after himself.'

'You're as sure of your position as he is of his.'

14

'I don't know. I'm not so sure. But, there's one thing I am sure about.'

'What's that?'

'We need a pint at the *Lion and Lamb*!'

'Who's the lion and who's the lamb?'

'Well tonight, if the lamb is sacrificial, it's definitely me!'

Questions for discussion

1. Who has the better of the argument between Tom and Adrian?

2. Do you agree with Alan that only those who believe in Christ can be saved? If not, how would you put it?

3. What do you say to those, like Tom, who find Christianity's emphasis on the death of Christ unhealthy and masochistic?

3

The Human Touch

Tom loved art. He had been to all the major European galleries, some of them many times. Rebecca, she was embarrassed to admit, had never in her twenty-four years even been to the National Gallery. This, then, was where Tom had brought her. His birthday present to her had been a study of Rembrandt about which he had been raving, and they now stood in front of the 1669 self-portrait, painted in the last year of Rembrandt's life. Tom talked about Rembrandt's failure to make a living, his debts, the death of both his wives, the criticism of his paintings by his contemporaries, the success of so many other artists who are now considered second-rate.

'Now,' he said, 'if you want to talk about justification, or salvation – I think that is what this painting is about. Here is someone who has seen the truth and seen it whole. He is under no illusions. But he is not full of self-pity either. He paints himself 'warts and all', weighing the failure, and just accepting it. I don't think you could say he "forgives himself". That just doesn't come into it. It's just a question of accepting the rough with smooth, and not being bitter about it.'

'But Rembrandt was a believer, wasn't he? He must have been. In that book you gave me there are amazing pictures of the crucifixion, and the most astonishing picture I've ever seen of the resurrection. You know, the supper at Emmaus. He was always doing religious paintings.'

'Well, yes he was. You could hardly not be in seventeenth-century Holland. But I don't think that was the heart of it. It seems to me that Rembrandt wasn't a religious painter. He was a humanist. He explores the depths of what it means to be human – the guile, the power, the failure, the sensuality, intelligence, stupidity – it's all there. I'm not sure he ever painted fanaticism, though, which he must have known about. But he didn't go to church much. Calvinism must have been too anti-humanist for him. You know that great poem of Edwin Muir, who knew Calvinism as well as Rembrandt did:

> The Word made flesh is here made word again
> in flourish and arrogant crook

– something like that.'

'Is that what you think about St Michael's?'

'Oh, no. That's different again. They're much too enthusiastic to be Calvinists. I can't imagine Rembrandt's contemporaries singing all those choruses, let alone doing sacred dance in church! No, I'm not trying to get at you. It's just that we've been talking a lot about "salvation", and you say that it's about being "made whole". Well, what I'm saying is that Rembrandt paints a "whole" person for us, whose wholeness comes precisely through failure, but I don't think it has much to do with religion, or "knowing Jesus", or believing that "Jesus died for me".'

'What do you think he's saying in his religious paintings, then? Surely, they're Christian paintings. Rembrandt is expressing his faith in them. He couldn't have painted the Supper at Emmaus unless he was.'

Tom paused. 'I agree,' he said slowly. 'It's not humanism and nothing but, is it? But isn't it something about the divine in human beings? When he paints Jesus, it's the humanity he's concerned about. It's not like the thirteenth-century paintings we saw twenty minutes ago. They painted the "God become man". Rembrandt painted the "man for others", didn't he? Perhaps he shared the views of his contemporary Spinoza, who was a pantheist, and saw God in everything. What I'm getting at is that his view of salvation is different. Did he even have one? Of course his contemporaries all did. They believed something like what Adrian believes, I suppose, and what you believe. But for Rembrandt "being made whole", it seems to me, is something that happens independently of a death on a

17

cross. Perhaps "the cross" becomes a metaphor for the suffering and failure which is part of the human lot. That's what schools us and "saves" us.'

'I'm not sure you're right. You know that picture of the Elevation of the Cross?'

'Yes, it's in Munich.'

'Yes, well, in the reproduction I saw, it shows Rembrandt himself putting the cross up, as if he himself is guilty of the crucifixion. I can't believe that comes out of the kind of humanism you're arguing for.'

'I think it does. He's looking back at us straight out of the picture, and challenging our complicity with evil. The cross is a metaphor for human evil.'

In the afternoon they crossed the river and went to see a performance of *King Lear*. That, too, provided food for thought and discussion. Tom argued that Shakespeare, like Rembrandt, was a humanist, whose religious beliefs were subordinate to his understanding of human good and evil.

'I don't know whether Shakespeare knew the ancient Greek view that tragedy was cathartic, but whether he did or not, that's the effect of his plays. They're pure catharsis. Purification through pity and terror. All of them have death, of course, but it's not a vicarious death. Or I suppose you could say that all of the deaths are "for us" in a sense. They hold up the mirror to ourselves and help us to be better people that way. It's all about self-realization. Learning to live with yourself and accept yourself. That's basically what salvation is.'

'But the characters are only fictions. They're not real people. You couldn't be saved by a fiction.'

'Why not?'

'Well, I know that in a sense the experience is real, but it's all in the realm of the mind and imagination, isn't it? It's not historically real, and that's what we need. Something which redeems the real historical world.'

18

'I have to say there isn't much evidence of Jesus doing that. OK, you have friends like Dawn, and that's impressive. But look at the history of Western Europe since it became Christian. It could hardly be bloodier, could it? And quite a lot of that bloodshed was directly the fault of the church – all the antisemitism, the crusades, the witch burnings, the wars of religion. It's not a very convincing picture of salvation, is it?'

'Of course, I grant you that. But what Adrian says is that there's a hidden history within history. There's the history of the wars and kings and armies and all that, and there's the history in which God is working his purposes out. We can't necessarily see that, but it's there all the same. And it's a history in which there are millions of people like Dawn, but also a history where there is some real progress. Take the abolition of slavery, for example. Wilberforce fought for that, and he did so out of Christian conviction.'

'So he may have done, but it was Christian conviction which inspired the Spanish and the Portuguese to go to Latin America and reduce the indigenous population to slavery.'

'Was it Christian conviction, or was it greed for gold, and for power?'

'OK, fair enough, but coming back to your point about imagination and what is really real. What difference would it make if Christ was a fictional character? I'm not saying that he was. But would it make a huge amount of difference? Isn't what you believe about salvation something like a myth? Myths aren't necessarily bad things. Plato taught truth through myth, and come to think of it, I suppose Jesus' parables aren't that far removed from myths either. Isn't all this stuff about the death of Christ really a myth about how we need to die to the bad things in our lives, and live to the good things?'

'But the difference from myth, as I understand it, is that in Christ God becomes human. You could have a story which said that, and that would be one thing. It might be a parable of the human condition. But what we believe, or what I believe at any rate, is that the Creator of the universe actually took flesh alongside of us, shared our condition, and then died the death of the worst kind of criminal. If that's true, then it says all sorts of amazing things about God. It shows that God is not just powerful, but also knows about weakness. It shows that God is in total solidarity with us. And Jesus died saying "Father, forgive them" – and I think Rembrandt understood that, by the way – and therefore broke the chain reaction of hatred, violence, more hatred, and more violence. He put a stop to that. He shows us it's not the way.'

'That's impressive. But it's rather different from "Jesus died for me", isn't it? And the problem is, it didn't put a stop to violence. It's going on at this moment. We haven't been saved from that chain reaction. It's perhaps the deepest law of human culture.'

'I hope it's not the deepest law of human culture. There are lots of other laws, like falling in love, and friendship, and creativity. I hope the deepest law of human culture is what produced Rembrandt or *King Lear*. But think of it. Let's assume the universe isn't an accident, and that we're not just going to burn up at some moment and leave not a trace behind. Let's assume it was created by a being we'll call "God". Then it makes a huge difference what kind of a being that is. And that's where the difference between myth and history comes in. If it's a myth then ultimately we're still on our own. But what we believe is that that historical figure, Jesus of Nazareth, lets us know what the Creator of the universe is really like, and therefore what our end will be.'

'You're still not out of the wood, because the history is so obscure. You told me to read the Gospels, and I did. I read Matthew. You've got beautiful bits, like the Sermon on the Mount, and you've got terrible bits, like the curses on the Pharisees. How much antisemitism have they been responsible for down the centuries, do you suppose?'

'I don't know. It's a terrible thought. But we're getting rather gloomy. You remember that lovely Renoir you showed me?'

'Yes.'

'What were they doing?'

'Eating.'

'Splendid idea. Where are you going to take me?'

Questions for discussion

1. Tom thinks 'salvation' is a matter of maturity, and taking the rough with the smooth without getting bitter. Would you challenge that view, and if so, how?

2. Can we be 'saved' in any way by fictional creations? If not, what problems are associated with the historical Jesus?

3. How do we deal with the violence involved in the history of Christianity?

4

A Disagreeable Encounter

Part of Tom's job was producing a play once a year. This year it was Ibsen's *Ghosts*. It ran for four nights, and Rebecca saw it twice, on the second night and the fourth. After the last performance there was a party for the cast and everyone involved in the production, and Rebecca was invited, as were many of Tom's colleagues. They were interested to meet her. They could see that this relationship was more serious than any before and they were interested to know why. Tom had had dozens of girlfriends, all good looking, and there had to be something more to this relationship than looks, though people who had seen them out together reported with a degree of envy that 'Tom had done his usual thing'.

Tom had to be here, there and everywhere at the party, and Rebecca was collared by one of his colleagues, whom she didn't find the most agreeable companion.

'How did you like the play?'

'I thought it was very well done. The two principals were excellent.'

'Yes. Ibsen clearly loathed the Christianity of his day. So utterly hypocritical and restrictive.'

'I don't know whether he did or not. You surely can't judge just from Pastor Manders.'

'No. But the world he wrote about was dominated by this gloomy Protestantism. Hell and damnation and all that sort of thing. Thank God for secularization. Christianity's so morbid.'

'I don't think it is.'

'No. You go to St Michael's, don't you?'

'Yes I do.'

'No offence, but I can't understand how any intelligent person can do it. I mean, the Cathedral, yes. There's the music and the beauty of the building, and the old Dean isn't totally impossible. I once heard him give a lecture on the novel which was quite interesting. But St Michael's. You're all fanatics aren't you?'

'Well, what do you think? I'm a member. Do I seem to be a fanatic?'

'No. But, well, narrow then. Don't you all believe that unless you go to St Michael's or some church like it you'll be damned?'

'Of course not.' But she blushed slightly as she remembered the discussion at the Emmaus group some months back.

'You see,' said her tiresome companion, who was clearly more than a little worse for wear, 'Jesus is all right. I've got no quarrel with Jesus. It's his followers, and what they've done with him. All this stuff about the Saviour dying for me, and his wounds, and being bathed in the blood. Its pathological. It's sick.'

Rebecca took the first opportunity to free herself, and couldn't help wondering to what extent this colleague represented reports of St Michael's Tom had given him. It was very late by the time they went home. Tom was high, and it was no time to talk. Some days later, however, she broached it with him.

'I had a most disagreeable conversation with one of your colleagues at the party.'

'Oh. Who was that?'

'I don't remember his name. He had glasses and an old check sports jacket.'

'That would be Philip – the Christian baiter. Was he on at you?'

'Yes. I thought maybe he was reporting things you'd said to him.'

'Like what?'

'Like everyone at St Michael's being a fanatic, and narrow, and so on.'

'Well he would hardly have got that from me, would he? Everyone?'

'No. OK. But as a report on St Michael's in general.'

'No, don't worry. He's famous for it. He hates evangelicals. In fact, he's an upside-down fundamentalist. He mirrors them in their passion and their narrowness.' A great load was lifted off Rebecca's mind. She felt happier than she had done for days.

'He said something interesting, though. He said he had no problem with Jesus, but only with what his followers had made of him.'

'Yes. It's the idea of Jesus as a great moral teacher. Gandhi had the same view.'

'Did he?'

'Oh yes, he did. Gandhi was brought up on the Sermon on the Mount. He always revered Jesus as a great teacher. He just couldn't accept him as a Saviour. I have to say, I've always felt like that myself.'

'But that makes no sense of the crucifixion and resurrection.'

'No, that's right. But then it's very difficult to make sense of the crucifixion and resurrection. You can think of Jesus as a martyr. That's all right. There were lots of martyrs in ancient times who met death calmly and without bitterness. But putting it all together and saying that Jesus is Son of God, or God incarnate. That's where the problem comes.'

'But, if Jesus is just a teacher, how is he different from Gandhi?'

'Good question. Perhaps he isn't. Both were martyrs. Both were non-violent. In fact, I suppose Gandhi was more committed to non-violence than Jesus. Jesus drove the moneychangers out of the temple. And the woes on the Pharisees are full of violence.'

'It still doesn't add up to me. I mean, Gandhi achieved Indian independence, and that was great, but no church follows from Gandhi.'

'That's one of his virtues. The world has enough religions as it is. And you can't say nothing follows from Gandhi. Martin

24

Luther King looked to him. So do lots of peace activists. So did people in the apartheid struggle.'

'But they looked to Jesus as well. Look at Desmond Tutu. I think what I want to say is that in the Gospels there's a kind of plus, an irreducible element, that the idea of sage and martyr doesn't cover. And what we call salvation is bound up with that. Gandhi sets Martin Luther King, and the rest of us, an example, but we don't learn from examples very well. We need more than that.'

'And what's that "more", do you think?'

'Well that's what we mean by talking about sacrifice and satisfaction. I agree with you that they are metaphors. But metaphors aren't just nothing. We use them to point to important things. In this case they say: this is bigger and heavier and weightier than a mere example.'

'Why do you say a "mere" example'? Surely, a truly good example is one of the things which makes the greatest impression on us. Aren't those of us in education committed to that?'

'I don't think we are. "Do as I say and not as I do" is always our bottom line.'

'Well, I suppose that's true.'

'It's the real evil in human history which has to be tackled. And that's what Christ does by offering his life.'

'I just don't see it. Nothing has changed. In the first century you had the Roman empire torturing and oppressing people, and calling it "peace", and today you have all the modern empires imposing "peace" by sub-machine guns and napalm. How has evil been defeated?'

'But things have changed. We've argued this out before. There has been moral progress.'

'In the concentration camps and Hiroshima, I suppose.'

'No, but in the end of slavery, and in changing attitudes to women and children. I mean, Philip was right. Ibsen's Norway was awful, and today, even if all that happens, we don't condone it any more. And the position of women has changed. A hundred years ago I couldn't have gone to university. My job would have been to get married and to breed.'

'What's that got to do with Christ as Saviour of the world?'

'Well, Jesus spoke of the kingdom as a mustard seed, growing into a mighty tree. Maybe the ideas of a different kind of society were always destined to take millennia. Maybe God is patient. Maybe that is the way he works.'

'How do you know he's a he?'

'I'm sure he's not a he. OK, maybe that's the way God works. Patiently. In and through history.'

'Through example?'

'OK. Also through example. But not just through example, but through grace.'

'And what's grace?'

'The power of God at work in the world, leading us to forgiveness, to truth, to justice.'

'If it was just a bit more powerful, it would be very convenient.'

'But then God would be a manipulator. And God is not. God respects us.'

'The hidden Persuader?'

'Oh, you're impossible. No, not like an advertising conman. But persuading us through truth, through the gospel. Which is why it's so important the gospel be preached.'

'And not propagandized.'

'Yes, OK, I agree with that. But look. I'm so relieved it was just Philip, and not you, talking the other day. And now I'm getting tired of this. Can we go for a coffee?'

Questions for discussion

1. How adequate is it to think of Jesus as a great moral teacher? If it is inadequate, as Rebecca argues, how do we go beyond it?

2. Do we need to talk about the Spirit when we speak of salvation? What role does the Spirit play in the process?

3. Can we think of salvation in connection with progress in human history, as Rebecca argues? If we can, how does the once for all event of the cross fit in with that. If not, what is God up to in history?

5

Breakdown

Tom was getting extremely tense and irritable because he hadn't seen Rebecca for weeks. One of her close friends at work, Louise, had gone off sick, and it had transpired, after more than a week, that she was undergoing a major nervous breakdown. In the old days she would have been hospitalized, but in this particular area there were no hospitals any longer – all of them had been closed. The idea was 'care in the community', which in this case meant the family, but they lived hundreds of miles away, and Louise had lived here for the past five years. Somebody had to look after her. Rebecca was still single and had fewer commitments than others. She virtually moved in.

No easy diagnosis of Louise's illness seemed forthcoming. The strain of teaching had undoubtedly brought it on, but she seemed just to have disintegrated. She was being treated by drugs, saw the doctor regularly, had regular visits from the psychiatric social worker, and went for psychotherapy twice a week. But she could do virtually nothing for herself and such conversation as she had often made little sense. Twice she was brought back by police when members of the public had become alarmed by her behaviour and had phoned them.

All this took its toll on Rebecca. She, too, missed seeing Tom, but she didn't complain about it as much as he did. The congregation of St Michael's was supportive. Friends from the church sometimes came and sat in for her, allowing her to go out, and to keep the concert engagements she was committed to. Her teaching was running on automatic pilot. All her energy was going elsewhere.

Weeks passed into months, and Louise slowly started to mend. The drugs were part of it, but Rebecca's quiet 'being around', coping with what was sometimes very disconcerting behaviour and conversation with a minimum of fuss, was probably more important still. In June Louise decided to take a month's holiday back at her parents home in the north of England. Rebecca was able to move back to her flat and to give her relationship with Tom a higher priority. One of the first things they did was to take the bus out to the country and go for a fifteen mile walk. It turned out to be twenty miles, but there was an immensely refreshing pub stop half-way. The walk gave them plenty of time to talk about the events of the past few months.

'I can't pretend to understand what has happened,' she said. 'I don't think the doctors know either. It's as if the whole person we knew, so full of vitality and fun, just fell apart.'

'Was there something which triggered it?'

'Not as far as I know. Nothing special, anyway. I think it was the strain of teaching. Quite a lot of teachers have breakdowns.'

'Oh, I know. It happened to one of our Geography people last year.'

'I'm sure the drugs are helping, but I'm not sure they are the real cure.'

'No, I doubt that as well. You remember what the doctor says in *Macbeth* (Rebecca didn't. She didn't even remember there *was* a doctor in *Macbeth*, but she let him go on): "More needs she the divine than the physician. God, God forgive us all. Look after her."'

'When does that come?'

'You remember. It's right at the end. Lady Macbeth is sleepwalking, and her nurse calls the doctor.'

'Oh yes, I remember. "Out, damned spot!" Yes, of course. But there's nothing like that in Louise's case. With Lady Macbeth it was guilt, wasn't it?'

'Of course. But I was thinking, today we would say "psychotherapist" rather than divine, wouldn't we? And I suppose the human mind is rather fragile. I was hearing something on the radio the other day, which said that one in four people would experience some form of mental illness during their lifetime.'

'Goodness!'

'Yes, it's sobering isn't it.'

'I wonder if the psychotherapist has taken over from the divine. Jesus healed. I suppose some of the stories in the Gospels are about mental illness. The story of Legion. I suppose today we would call that schizophrenia. And our church has healing services. I know that faith can heal.'

'Did you take Louise to one.'

'No, I didn't. Like you, she's not a Christian, and if I'd done it whilst she was so confused, I would have felt I was taking advantage of her.'

'Isn't it superstition? These days it's the doctors we have to rely on.'

'But you yourself have just quoted the doctor in Macbeth. No, I don't think it's superstition. People are so complex, and who knows what's going on when the mind gets ill.'

'So what goes on in your healing services?'

'Actually, they're quite low key, and no one could think of them as superstitious. The Rector, or Adrian, or whoever happens to be taking the service, together with one or two members of the congregation, invite those who would like to come for healing, to come up to the altar. They lay their hands on them, and pray for their healing. Then the roles are reversed. Those who have had hands laid on them in turn lay their hands on those who prayed for their healing, and the same prayers are said. It's an acknowledgment that we're all broken and that we all need healing.'

'Have you done it?'

'Often.'

'But then doesn't that water down the meaning of what we mean by healing? I mean, if anyone's sound in mind and body you are!'

'No, I don't think it does. Actually you should approve, because it challenges the "reigning individualism" which you are always going on about. We say, "We are all members one of another."'

'"We" meaning?'

'Christians. But you believe it as well. Take Louise's illness. You can say it's just her problem, her illness. But I doubt it. Isn't her illness a symptom of the sickness of society at large? And doesn't the whole of society need healing?'

'Yes, it does. But that can't happen until we have got rid of capitalism.'

'Oh, get real, Tom. You know that's not going to happen for hundreds of years.'

'I know no such thing. I give it another fifty.'

'Well, however that may be, we've got Louise to deal with right here and now, and we can't abolish capitalism overnight. And anyway, the story of Legion shows that there was mental illness long before capitalism.'

'Another empire with a pathology of violence, though.'

'Stop changing the point. The point is that we need resources of healing, and I believe St Michael's is right, that that's available in the gospel.'

'We've had this out before. Nowhere do you find a higher concentration of pathologies than in religion. If you don't believe me, look at Northern Ireland.'

'That's not just about religion, and you know it. But, OK, let's concede your point. Isn't that just what you expect. Sick people seek a doctor. Where salvation is at hand, there the sick come.'

'Who's talking about salvation?'

'We are. Salvation comes from *salus* meaning health. You've forgotten your Latin.'

'I never had any Latin. I'm a school drop out, remember?'

'Well, it does. And going back to your quotation from *Macbeth*, I think it's a real question whether "salvation", or health, comes from the doctor or healers of souls.'

31

'You'll be telling me to go to the witch doctor next.'

'Tom, that's unfair. What I'm saying, as you know very well, is that there's a depth to human health and sickness which isn't just met by conventional medicine. Lots of doctors acknowledge that. We've got doctors in our congregation who come to the healing service, and think it's a very good thing.'

'OK. What I can see is that the improvement in Louise is certainly to do with your being around for the past few months. And my bad temper the past few months is to do with your not being around.'

'Poor you. But think of all the arguments its saved you.'

'It's the arguments I miss. But meanwhile, I think we'd better stop and take a compass reading. We've completely lost the path, and I've booked a table at the *Six Bells* for seven o'clock. I can vouch for the healing qualities of their beer!'

Questions for discussion

1. How important is physical and mental healing as part of salvation?

2. If Rebecca is right that some sickness is a symptom of a sick society, what are the implications of that for Christian discipleship?

6

A Visitor from El Salvador

Tom surprised Rebecca. He invited her to come to a theology lecture! He'd seen a poster advertising a lecture on liberation theology and thought it looked interesting. Six months ago he would never even have noticed a poster advertising anything to do with theology, but love does strange things.

The meeting was held in the rather tatty, and very crowded, main room of the local Dominican house. It had been arranged by the resident 'Justice and Peace' group. That in itself made Rebecca think. St Michael's didn't have one of those. The lecturer came from El Salvador. He spoke about the history of the country from ancient times, but especially since the Spanish occupation in the sixteenth century. He talked about the way a few families owned virtually all of the land, about the poverty of the peasantry, high mortality and poor education. He then talked about the struggle between left-wing guerrillas and the Arena government, which lasted twenty years, a struggle in which 60,000 people died, mostly peasants, though including some Jesuits, secular clergy, and nuns. He talked about torture, including of children. He told the story of a nine-year-old girl who, before she died, had her tongue cut out, and her hands chopped off, for belonging to a family which opposed the government. He told how the Arena government had been funded by the US government, and how Britain had been a major arms supplier. Then he talked about liberation theology. He spoke of Vatican II and the new initiatives, of the rise of a new theology, biblically based, and attempting to relate to the peasantry, in the whole of Latin America. He said that clergy, appalled by the suffering of the poor, had realized with a new force that the gospel could not be just otherworldly, but related to things here and now. He spoke of the struggle for political freedoms, for better living conditions, for education. The church, he said, was concerned with 'integral human

33

liberation'. This included spirituality, but not to the exclusion of material matters.

When he finished, Tom was the first to put a question. 'You've spoken a lot about liberation,' he said, 'but you haven't mentioned salvation. In this country it's usually the other way round. Could you comment on that, please?'

The speaker laughed. He was used to the question. 'I won't comment on your situation,' he said, 'but for us, see, the whole point is that for centuries the church preached an otherworldly gospel – pie in the sky when you die. And it preached devotion to the Virgin and the saints – and people accepted it. They were told that those who were poor in this world would get their reward hereafter. And that's the way we priests were trained as well. We were taught to hear confession, and say mass, and to be chaplains to the men's groups and the women's groups.

'But then, when we started to read the Bible with fresh eyes we saw that this wasn't right. The Bible wasn't an otherworldly book. It was a book about this world. We had ignored most of Scripture! We read Deuteronomy, we read Leviticus, we read Exodus, we read the prophets, and we said, "Hey, is this the Word of God or not? If it's the Word of God we'd better get our act together."

'And of course, there was opposition. People said we weren't supposed to be that concerned with the Old Testament but only with the New. But that's not what was coming out of Vatican II. And in any case, we were learning to read the New Testament differently. We had read it as a book about the teaching of Jesus, the sufferings of Jesus, and the resurrection which confirmed God's seal of approval on those sufferings. Then our theologians started to talk about eschatology. They said the New Testament was all about eschatology, and that wasn't about the end of the world, but about hope, here and now. And we looked at Luke's Gospel – you know, the passage in chapter 4 where Jesus quotes Isaiah, and says, "The Spirit of the Lord is upon me, because he has anointed me to bring good news to the poor . . . to proclaim release to the captives . . . to let the oppressed go free." And we said, "That's what we should be doing! We are continuing the task of Jesus. His teaching was centred on the kingdom, and it was a kingdom of justice and peace. He inaugurated it, but it is still to come, and we have to work towards its coming." Not that we will bring it. We can't do that. God will bring it. But meanwhile we can't be idle. We have been given the Nazareth manifesto, and we have to live by it.

'And so you ask about the difference between salvation and liberation. See, my friend, of course we need salvation from sin. I agree. But sin isn't only about what you do in your bedroom or your office. It affects the whole of society, and we need freeing from it. Hence "liberation".'

Another man at once stood up at the back of the room. 'It's all very well you talking about the Bible,' he said, 'but I think you're misleading us. You have been criticized by the present Pope, and if my memory serves me right the Vatican commissioned a critique of your type of theology, and it said that you're not really biblical at all, but Marxist. All this talk about the Bible obscures the real agenda, which is communism. And communism doesn't work. It's evil. It failed in Eastern Europe, and it will always fail. It ignores the fact of sin. And that seems to me what you are doing.'

The speaker smiled. He was used to this accusation as well. 'My friend,' he said, 'let me make a confession. I have read Karl Marx, and I continue to read him. I wonder how much of Marx you have read yourself. But I don't believe in Marx. I believe in the Holy Trinity, Father, Son and Holy Spirit. When I say mass, I pray to the Father, through the Son, in the Spirit. That's my faith. Now I read Marx. Of course I do. I read lots of people: Pablo Neruda, Isabel Allende, Cervantes, even some of your own authors. I've read Shakespeare – in translation. As well as Marx I read other sociologists – Weber, and Durkheim, and contemporary writers like Manuel Castells. I don't have a list of proscribed books. Once I even read *Mein Kampf.* It doesn't make me a Nazi. OK, I read Marx more seriously than I read Hitler. Why? Because what he was attempting to do was to understand capitalism, and we live under a capitalist system. I want to try and understand how profits accrue, what drives big business, which is controlled by the rich in our country. And I find him illuminating. He helps me to understand what's going on, especially in what he says about commodity fetishism.'

'About what?' interjected another member of the audience.

'Marx said that under capitalism all relationships become "commodified", mediated by money. And he saw that was a form of fetishism, a form of idolatry. Idolatry is worship of something we make ourselves, and in capitalism the thing that we worship is money. Now Marx wasn't a Christian, but any Christian knows that we are fundamentally opposed to idolatry. We can worship only the living God. But Marx helps me to understand how our society is basically idolatrous. As a Christian I want to turn it away from idols to worship of the living God.'

Sitting near the front was a man in battered fatigues. He spoke with a strong American accent. It turned out he was an American Dominican who had spent a lot of time in Latin America.

'We like to talk about this,' he said, 'in the language of the principalities and powers. Lots of people think that's myth, but it's not. The principalities and powers are real. That language is a way of talking of the spiritual interiority of things. In the book of Revelation it's applied to churches, but you can apply it to cultures, and nations, and movements as well. Every culture has its spiritual interiority, and that's a tremendous power. You have to be an exceptional individual to resist it. The book of Daniel talks about the angels of the nations. That's the same thing. And there, the angels resist God for days on end. Well, forget days. We're talking centuries. The principalities and powers are the sedimentation of human choices of power and every anti-life force, built up over hundreds of years into a thick sludge. Only sludge isn't the right word for it. It's something active, which embraces us and leads us on crusade. And today, capitalism is one of those powers. And they don't come as angels of darkness. Oh no. They're much more subtle than that. They come as an angel of light. All that killing and torture in Latin America, that was done in the name of freedom, and justice, and even of the gospel. But of course, the gospel is the challenge to these spiritualities of death. Christ unmasks them. He reveals them for what they are. He enables us to read history with eyes which aren't blinded by their subtle propaganda. He enlists us on the side of life. Not in a crusade. No crusade can ever be Christian. But as peace activists of the kingdom. Challenging the might of the powers.'

The speaker was being dined after the meeting, but Tom and Rebecca got talking to the American and found that he was free, and invited him to join them down at the pub. His name was Bill. They learned that he had been in Britain for over a year on a placement within his order. He was longing to get back to Latin America, though unusually for a North American he had no complaints about the British weather, British food, or even British beer, about which he was quite a connoisseur. He had not worked in El Salvador, but he had lots to tell them about Guatemala, Nicaragua and Peru, where he had worked.

'I had no idea that was all going on as I was growing up,' said Rebecca. 'I suppose I was a very sheltered child.'

'No,' said Tom, 'the media over here just aren't interested. It's the latest stories on *Neighbours* or about the Spice Girls which make the news, not children murdered in Latin America.'

Bill said the North American media were just the same.

'But Bill,' said Rebecca, 'isn't there some point to the Vatican objections. I still wonder whether what you call liberation theology doesn't make the gospel too political. I mean, even amongst the poor and oppressed personal faith must count. Even the poor sin. They need redemption too. Somehow reducing the idea of salvation to liberation seems a bit impoverished to me. In the church I come from the gospel is always preached in terms of justification, and surely that's an aspect we just can't eliminate.'

'I agree,' said Bill. 'But you see, you've got to understand justification rightly. A lot of our problems with it come from the time the New Testament was translated into Latin. The Greek word *dikaiosune* was translated by *justificatio*, which gave a completely different colour to the word. The Roman genius was forensic: they loved sorting things out in court. One of their greatest writers, Cicero, was an advocate, what you people over here would call a QC. It was natural for them to think in legal terms, and that way of thinking passed down into the church, where we developed canon law, and had church courts and all the rest of it. But though Paul was a Roman citizen, he had a Hebrew mindset. And when he said "righteousness" he wasn't thinking "law court", he was thinking Isaiah. Isaiah's the prophet of righteousness in the Hebrew Bible, and for him it means God seeing that the right is maintained, and that means that the poor are defended and the rich don't get away with blue murder. Have a look in the opening chapters of Isaiah when you get home.

'But what you say about the poor is of course right. If the tables were turned, if they suddenly became rich and the rich poor, would they behave any better? I doubt it. So, yes, they sin, as we all do, and they certainly do need redemption. But the point of liberation theology is this: it takes the body seriously. It's not satisfied with the salvation of the soul. It wants the salvation of the whole person – body, mind and spirit. Now lots of Christians go along with that, and recognize that, in the debate on pornography. Fine, I agree with them. But they don't go on to extend it to houses, and sewage, and schools and hospitals. And that's what we do. But as soon as you do that, people start shouting "communist" – especially in the United States. It's not so bad over here.'

'I have to admit,' said Tom, 'that I'm not a Christian, but what you say makes a lot of sense to me. What's that book you say we ought to read? I'm ashamed to say I've never read the Bible. Only bits of the New Testament.'

'No need to be ashamed. Lots of people haven't read the Bible. The highest selling book in the world, and the least read. Isaiah. Try chapters one to five.'

Walking home, Tom and Rebecca continued talking about the individual and society. 'It seems to me,' said Tom, 'that your lot are too focussed on the individual, and isn't that an abstraction? We're not individuals, are we? We all exist in and through relationships.'

'Of course we are. Which reminds me. You're meant to be meeting my family on Saturday. Are you still OK for that?'

Questions for discussion

1. To what extent are liberation and salvation different and to what extent the same?

2. Where does language about 'the kingdom' fit in with thought about salvation?

3. What do you make of Bill's talk about 'the powers'?

7

Out of the Depths

Rebecca had, of course, not stopped going to St Michael's, but she went somewhat less often than she used to. It wasn't just that she and Tom were forever going places at weekends, but she had also become a regular at the prison, and liked to go to the weekly eucharist there. Somehow she found she could cope with Fr David's vestments and his high church ways, when previously she had always been allergic to them. She had also become a prison visitor. She was a good listener, had a lot of common sense, and her visits cheered people up. That was why Fr David decided he would ask her to visit Jason. Jason had been on rule 2052 – suicide watch – for some days.

She sat in the interview room, with its Formica table and tubular chairs, for some time before Jason came in, head bowed and shoulders stooped. He sat down in silence. The warder signed that he would wait immediately outside the door. After a short pause she offered Jason a cigarette. She did not smoke herself, but found it useful to take a packet of cigarettes in with her. Jason took deep pulls on the cigarette without looking at her, but looking somewhere down through the middle of the table.

'Jason,' she said, 'I don't want to force you to speak. If you want we can just sit here in silence, and that's OK. But I'd like to hear what you're thinking.'

'I can't.'

'You can't?'

'I can't talk about it. It's no use.'

A longish silence followed. 'Try talking about it.'

Slowly Jason started to blurt out his story, very disjointedly, repeating himself sometimes. As he went on he gained impetus. His mother had died a few weeks ago, whilst he was inside. There had been no one to tell him that she was even ill, and he hadn't got to see her. She was the only person he was really

attached to, the only person who in any way believed in him.
He'd never been successful. His Dad had left home when he
was three, and he had no memories of him. He'd failed at
school. He'd got casual work as a building labourer, and never
earned very much. Arguments at home led him to try and live
away from home, but that was never very successful either.
Girlfriends hadn't worked out, and he had no mates whom he
could look to. Drinking alone in a pub one night he'd set off to
drive back home, come round a bend too fast, and gone head on
into another car. He was four times over the limit. He escaped
with cuts and bruises, but the young couple in the other car had
both died. He was charged with causing death by dangerous
driving and got three years. He was sorry about the death of the
young couple, but had no idea how to say so. Their families
were bitter. They had shouted at him in court. Not knowing
how to deal with it he'd turned in on himself. His only visitor
had been his Mum, weary and dogged, with little scraps of
news and kindness. And now she was gone, with no farewells,
no final words. Life had collapsed around him. He wished he'd
died, and not the young couple. He wished he'd died before his
Mum. There was nothing for him but death. There was no other
prospect.

Rebecca knew what her St Michael's training required her to
say. 'God loves you.' Could she say it? Wouldn't it just be
empty words? Her mouth was dry.

'Jason, I want to say something to you. You seem absolutely
alone, but you're not. God loves you. He loves you just as you
are. He has a future for you, though you can't believe it now.
He knows you're sorry about what happened, and he forgives
you. And he'll find something for you when you come out.
Life's not at an end.'

There was silence. 'I don't know about God. I only know
about hell.'

'I know you do. I can see. But God isn't absent even from
hell. He's there. He knows about it. And he knows about you.

41

No one is Godforsaken. You think you are, but you're not. Look, Jason, I want to suggest something. I want to go and meet those families. I want to bring them here to meet you. I think if you can meet them, that will bring you out of hell.'

'They won't come.'

'They might. Can I ask them?'

'It's no use.'

'Can I try?'

'If you want.'

Outside the prison Rebecca was surprised at herself. It wasn't many months ago that she believed hell was the absence of God, and that unbelievers were either there or on their way there. What had happened to her? Why had she said God was present even in hell?

Fr David had given her the address of the two families. Should she ring them up, or write to say she was coming? She asked Tom. He said it was probably best just to turn up unannounced, because otherwise they would make excuses not to see her. He offered to drive her to the two homes – only a mile or so apart – and to wait for her while she went in to speak with them. Neither family was easy. From the first she was turned away with bitter words as a 'do gooder' who couldn't possibly understand. But the girl's family listened, and finally agreed to come to the prison. They fixed a date for the visit.

Tom had agreed to come with her to pick up the girl's parents and bring them to the prison. He stayed outside whilst Rebecca and the parents went in to see Jason. They were gone about an hour, and then drove back and went in for a cup of tea. They were grateful. They thought it had helped. It didn't bring their daughter back, but they understood now that Jason was neither wicked nor simply careless. He'd said repeatedly that he'd wished it had been him, and they could see that he meant it. Somewhere in the awkward words and the grieving were the germs of forgiveness and reconciliation and of new life for Jason.

It made a difference to Jason, too. Two days after the visit he came off 2052 and back to a normal regime. Rebecca arranged to see him after work. His first question was about the parents. He asked persistently about how they were feeling, and seemed to be reassured. Then he said, 'You know what you said, about being Godforsaken. You were right. That's just what I did feel. And I feel much better now. I don't feel alone in the same way any more.'

'I'm glad.'

'Do you think it's God?'

'God's presence you mean? Yes I do.'

'I'm sorry about the parents. I'm sorry. I'm really sorry.'

'I know. And they know so too.'

'Do you think they'll ever forgive me?'

'I think they might, with time.'

'Only, I want a new future. With good conduct I can be out in a year and a half. Do you think I can find a job?'

'I'm sure you can.'

'Thanks for coming.'

'No problem, I'm glad you're feeling better.'

On the way home Rebecca was both deeply relieved and apprehensive at the same time. What if he didn't find a job? She understood the difficulties only too well. Forgiveness was the breakthrough, but there was no salvation for Jason without a job either. But at least they had a little time to work on it.

Questions for discussion

1. Many people feel Godforsaken, as Jason did. What are other reasons for that feeling, and how should we address it?

2. How do you convey the reality of God's presence to someone who claims that God means nothing for them?

3. Rebecca believes that there is no 'salvation' for Jason without a job. Is this too strong a use of the term 'salvation'? If not, what are the implications for our church life?

8

Josef

Tom was not the kind of person for whom an evening away from the pub was wasted time, but on the other hand he appreciated good ale and good company. The *Lion and Lamb* was owned by its publican, who brewed his own beer on the premises. It had no jukebox, and no piped music, and all the original Victorian snugs were in place, six rooms in all. One of the regulars at the pub was Josef, an old man, now in his eighties, and he and Tom were good friends.

Josef had been in Auschwitz, and still had his camp number tattooed on his left wrist. He'd been born in Lodz, and had lost his entire family in the camps. He was fourteen when the camp was liberated, and had set off with a group of other survivors to get to Israel. Somehow he got separated from them on a crowded, chaotic station in Central Europe, missed his train, and got in with another group of refugees and soldiers, and found himself after four days, with only a pass stamped by the American military, in Dover. Alone in Dover, without a word of English, he'd been 'adopted' by a large cheery woman whose surname, to his immense confusion at first, was Halfpenny, who lived on her own in a caravan to the north of the town. She knew only one thing about Jews: that they were tailors, something she'd heard from cousins in the East End. She accordingly apprenticed Josef to a tailor, and as such he'd made his living. She never formally adopted him, but he became Joe Halfpenny, though to his friends he always remained Josef. He'd married, and had children, but his wife had died before him. Though he'd come to England at fourteen, and spent all his life there, his East European accent was still audible. He was to be found most evenings sitting quietly in the *Lion and Lamb*. He spoke relatively little about the war, but people knew his story, and he and Tom, in particular, had very 'deep' conversations.

On one of their evenings at the pub Tom introduced Josef to Rebecca. Conversation meandered for a while, until Rebecca asked if Josef ever went to synagogue.

'Last time I went to a synagogue was . . . it must have been 1943. Our last days in the ghetto. My father always insisted.'

'You never went after you came to England?'

'No.'

Rebecca did not like to pursue the question, and other topics came up, but after a while Josef said, 'Tom tells me you're a believer. I'm not a believer. I *was*. As a boy I was very pious. I even wanted to be a Rabbi. But my God died in the camps. After that I couldn't believe. No God. There couldn't be a God. If there was a God, things like that wouldn't happen – killing children, throwing them into pits. I don't know. Maybe there was a God. But if so, he died.'

Rebecca swallowed. She had no idea what to say. She could not even say 'I understand,' because she did not understand. Thinking about it she found herself close to tears.

Tom could see what was going on, and intervened.

'No, I agree. We've often said this, and that's why I agree with you, Josef. Things would have to be very different to be able to believe in God. But you often say you envy those who can believe.'

'I envy those who can believe. I do. It makes life simpler and it makes life harder, but there it is.'

Later, sitting in Rebecca's tiny kitchen, drinking coffee, they talked it over. 'Of course I understand,' Rebecca was saying. 'If I were in his place, I would feel the same. But if there ever was a God, he couldn't have died. That's a strange idea. Adrian was talking about this sort of thing last Good Friday. I wish I could remember what he said. It was something about "the crucified God". He quoted from a book by someone else who had been in the camps. He said God was there, alongside those who were suffering. I can't remember all the details, but it was something about God's solidarity with the victims. I know it impressed me deeply at the time.'

'If there was a God, wouldn't you expect something more than solidarity? You were telling me last week that the name Jesus means "God saves", but God didn't, did he?'

'No,' she said hesitantly.

'Well, six million dead doesn't say much for solidarity, does it?'

'But wait a minute. What you're expecting from God is for him to come in like Superman when things go wrong. The whole point of the cross is that he can't do that.'

'Go on.'

'It's something about God respecting our freedom, and something about creation and the nature of love. I mean, if I love you, I can't force you to do something.'

'No, but when you love someone, and you see them being attacked, you intervene.'

'But if you're God, could you intervene and still let people have freedom? If God intervened like that, then we would all be puppets, and puppets can't love. And if that's the case, then what is God to do about that kind of wickedness and suffering? Lots of people think of God as remote and above the fray. But that's not what we read in the Bible. God is passionate – gets wounded, and hurt. And that's what the incarnation is about. It's the expression of God's love. And when it's rejected God doesn't intervene in the way that you want him to. That question was raised then, now I come to think of it. When Jesus was crucified those who were around were taunting him saying, "Come down off the cross and save yourself!" So it's the same kind of thing. God intervenes, but only by putting himself alongside the victims. It's about the expression of God's love.'

'It's a peculiar kind of love which ends up in the gas chambers.'

'I agree. But what's the alternative? According to you, this life is all there is. We die, and that's it. If there's no redemption

47

at the end of the day, then I don't think our lives, or history, or the whole universe make sense.'

'"Evolutionary accidents crawling about on a cooling cinder", is what Bertrand Russell called us.'

'Well, there you are.'

'But maybe he's right.'

'Yes, and then the Gestapo were the victors. I don't believe that. I think there will be vindication for the gassed and the tortured one day.'

'Isn't that pie in the sky?'

'What are you offering? Pie for the fortunate few?'

'No. But it's what Camus says. We have to think clearly, and not hope any more.'

'We can't live without hope. We have to have hope. Life without hope is no life.'

'Plato said an unexamined life was no life.'

'Did he? Well, I think hope is more important.'

'But without critical examination of things you can just slip into sentimentality. It's Disneyfication.'

'What do you mean by that?'

'Reducing everything to the level of a Disney film.'

'And is that what you think I'm doing?'

'Not at all.'

'Well then.'

'Well then what?'

'Well then. The hope of resurrection isn't Disneyland. It's hope for justice at the end of the day. And, OK, maybe it's a tall order, but I don't see that it's so utterly absurd. It's grounded in the Gospels, and they're not fairy stories, but rather sober and hard headed stories which wrestle with tragedy and death and suffering and don't give any easy answers.'

'You don't think resurrection is an easy answer?'

'Not at all. Hope against hope, I think Paul calls it. It's faith in the teeth of so much of the evidence. But it's faith to live by all the same. I don't say I blame Josef for not having it. I don't.

But I can't surrender it myself, even in the face of that kind of terrible story.'

There was a silence. Tom took Rebecca's hands. 'Good,' he said. 'I don't want you to.'

Questions for discussion

1. Does salvation for the victims of the terror of history involve belief in God? Is it not enough just to remember them? If not, why not?

2. Christians believe in redemption, but how do they avoid palming people off with glib and easy answers?

3. Where does the resurrection fit in with our beliefs about salvation?

9

A Feminist Theologian

At the liberation theology meeting Tom and Rebecca had put their names down for mailings on forthcoming events. Several events had come and gone and they hadn't been able to attend for one reason or another, but now there was a speaker on feminist theology whom they were both keen to hear. Same time, same place, only now it was summer, and the creaky radiators were no longer on, and the windows were open, and evening sunlight streamed into the hall. The speaker was introduced as a leading British feminist theologian. She had been asked to assume no knowledge, which indeed in Tom's case was absolutely right, so she began with the traditional position of women in the church. She said something about the role of Mary in Catholic piety right up to the present. Then she began with the rise of the first feminist movement in the eighteenth century, with Mary Wollstonecraft, and later the suffragettes, and came down to the more recent past, with 'second wave feminism', and the theological response to that.

Many of the questions were about women priests, and most from a specifically Catholic perspective. But when there was a lull in the questioning Rebecca asked if the speaker could say something about a feminist perspective on salvation.

'Thank you for that,' said the speaker. 'That's a very helpful question. As you've already seen, feminists don't all agree with one another. I would say that there are two broad strands – apart today from what the papers are calling "bimbo feminism". That's the Spice girls and all that, and I don't know whether that's feminism at all really.

'Anyway, there's a strand of what we can call "equality feminism", which believes that men and women are the same in all important respects, except that women have traditionally got far fewer of the top jobs. And then there's "difference feminism", and the classic text for that is a book by Carol

Gilligan called *In a Different Voice*. That argues that men and women have distinctively different ways of approaching things, and that women are much more focussed on relationships and on reconciliation than men are. Men tend to be confrontational. Traditionally, anyway, they wanted to sort things out by a sock on the jaw. If you look at road rage incidents, it's nearly always men isn't it? If they think their ego has been challenged by another man they get out and stalk round to the other car looking for a fight. Women sort things out by talking things through.

'In traditional societies women have often been healers, and I think that gives us a clue. You might say that the traditional male idea of redemption is the cosmic battle: good versus evil. El Alamein in heaven. Look how Milton enjoys the battle scenes in *Paradise Lost*. But a feminist perspective on redemption will think much more of healing broken relationships. It's a whole different mindset. On the one hand, when something's wrong you think of taking up arms. As Goebbels said, "You reach for your gun". On the other hand you say, This is a wound. Someone's hurt. Let's see if we can heal them.

'Now of course, it's important to learn from Jung here. Jung said that we all have male and female sides to our characters. There are men who have a very feminine side, and women who can be "macho". But ask yourself where Jesus stands. It seems to me, when you look at the Gospels, that the feminine side of his nature is very strongly developed. After all, one of the things we know most certainly about him is that he was a healer. He likes sitting and talking to people. He likes listening. He plays with children. He likes the company of women, but clearly without any erotic intent. There's no hint of that in the Gospels.

'Traditionally Christians have understood their vocation in terms of the imitation of Christ. As I understand it, that means imitation of this deeply "feminine" figure. Christ just isn't a

51

typical "macho male". The New Testament writers use imagery from Isaiah 53 to talk about him: they compare him to a lamb, a servant. Well, who were servants in antiquity? Who are servants now? Who's making the coffee tonight?'

A burly Dominican with a Desperate Dan stubble said 'I am', to general laughter.

'I take your point,' said Rebecca, 'but how do we think of that in terms of the traditional images of salvation. When you go into a church, after all, what you see is an image of the cross. How does that fit in with your healing of wounds?'

'I think in two ways. First of all, you can think of the cross as a battle, and many of the ancient writers did. We sing during Holy Week:

> Sing, my tongue, the glorious battle,
> Sing the ending of the fray.

But there's another way of thinking of it. Jesus died forgiving those who had crucified him. Now what that does, to my way of thinking, is to break the chain of aggression. It's precisely not a battle, where blow is followed by counter blow. As Isaiah put it: "He hid not his face from shame and spitting." That's not masochism. On the contrary, it's a recognition that fighting gets you nowhere.

'But then you can ask, well what follows from that? And this is crucial I think. After the crucifixion comes the resurrection, and then comes Pentecost. Think of it like this: The crucifixion is throwing the stone into the pool, and Pentecost is the ripples going on out and out and out. Only you need to change the metaphor to think of the ripples actually accomplishing something. I think what it's about is this. We say that the incarnation is God's involvement in history. And so it is. But it doesn't stop at the ascension. The church is the register of that impact on history, continuing it, continuing the praxis of reconciliation – Matthew says, until the end of time. And that's what we're involved in. It's a question of healing the world's wounds, restoring relationships where they've been broken and damaged.'

'But you yourself have said,' interposed another woman, 'that the church betrays Jesus' intentions.'

'Of course it does. It always did. Think of Peter. The church began with betrayal. But it's not only betrayal. There's faithfulness in the midst of unfaithfulness, and loyalty in the midst of disloyalty. And that is still true. And so I think we must talk of a redemptive, reconciling, healing *process.* Salvation is not just a once for all event. It is that. But it's also a process, a movement, in which we are part.'

Tom and Rebecca walked home through the park. It was the most beautiful evening.

'I think what she said made a lot of sense,' said Tom.

'Good. So did I.'

'I think she'd have a lot to teach your Adrian, and the Emmaus group.'

'H'm. Yes. It's a pity they don't come to these kind of events. They're still so suspicious of Catholics.'

'The real problem is, isn't it, that they think they have all the answers?'

'Oh, I don't know about that. Don't run them down. There are a lot of good people there too.'

'Well, yes, I'm sure there are. But I tell you what.'

'You're ready for some refreshment.'

'How did you guess?'

Questions for discussion

1. Does feminism have a distinctive contribution to make to our thinking about redemption? If so, how would you characterize it?

2. To what extent must we think of salvation in terms of the restoration of right relations between people?

3. If the speaker is right, and we have to think of salvation as a process, then what follows from that for our Christian discipleship?

10

A Harvest Sermon

The wedding had been wonderful. It had taken place at St Michael's, but Fr David had presided and preached. All their friends had come, even Philip, who had given them the most marvellous coffee maker, 'to stir you up, make you argumentative, and keep you awake at night,' as he said. They had, of course, long ago ceased to be 'Tom and Rebecca' to any of their friends, but were universally known as 'Music and Drama'. A long search for accommodation had produced somewhere on the edge of town, near woods and fields. They knew that children might force a rethink, particularly because the house was small, but for the moment they were both fit enough to cycle the four miles to work, and enjoy it. Their churchgoing habits were shockingly eclectic. By and large they supported the local church, still recognizably a 'village' church, even though the village was by now to all intents and purposes part of the town. They brought the average age of the congregation down by about forty years! But they also went to mass at the jail from time to time, and sometimes to the Dominican house, whilst they had also become great friends with the Methodist minister, who was a neighbour. Tom still described himself as an agnostic, but churchgoing was not a chore, and Rebecca's faith no embarrassment.

Stephen, the Methodist minister, had been a plant scientist before changing jobs in mid-career. He was a passionate environmentalist, a 'Green' councillor, and always in demand to talk about GM crops, the ozone layer, the effects of global warming, road building, and so on. He was an enthusiast for Celtic Christianity which, he felt, took the doctrine of creation seriously in a way that traditional Western Christianity had by and large failed to do.

It was harvest time, and the local churches decided to pool resources rather than run competing events. Harvest festival,

55

still a big event in the 'village', would be held in the old
church, but the Rector left both service and sermon to Stephen,
recognizing that this was very much his area of expertise.

Stephen chose to preach on Romans 6.1–2: 'Should we
continue in sin in order that grace may abound? By no means!
How can we who died to sin go on living in it?'

'I bet you think that's a rum text for a harvest sermon,' he
began. 'And it seems to be at first sight. But I hope by the time
I've finished you'll see it makes sense.

'As you all know, in Genesis we're given dominion over
creation. God says: "Have dominion over the fish of the sea,
and over the birds of the air and over every living thing that
moves upon the earth." For centuries we have abused that text.
Human beings behaved as if that made them *conquistadors*,
who could burn and rape and plunder. Technology was based
on mining – extracting without putting anything back. Today
we live with the results of that. Growing holes in the ozone
layer, so that ultra-violet radiation isn't filtered out, which
means in turn that coral reefs are crashing, and with them
plankton, which could pose a threat to all life. The destruction
of forests, driven by the need to earn foreign exchange, and by
the search of logging companies for quick profits. That in turn
drives global warming, which threatens not just small island
republics in the Pacific, and Bangladesh, but the east coast of
England.

'God didn't put us here to abuse creation, but to live in
relationship to it. Instead of mining, a much better model for
our relationship to creation is farming. I'm not talking about
agribusiness, which is also extractive, but the kind of farming
which has been practised round here for at least a millennium.
The basic rule of farming is rotation. You have to give the land
a rest from time to time. That was recognized in the Old
Testament in extending the sabbath both to land and to beasts.
Any dairy farmer will tell you that a cow is not a machine.
She'll only do her best for you if you treat her properly.

56

'Now perhaps you're thinking I've picked up the wrong script this evening. That instead of the sermon I picked up a political address. If that's what you think you've got another think coming, because I'm not talking here about agriculture and the environment. I'm talking about sin and salvation. How come?

'Well, sin is the name we give to behaviour which destroys the good earth which God has given us. At harvest time we give thanks to God for all his gifts. The Latin word for "gratitude" is *gratia*, grace. Grace isn't just about the power of God redeeming us, as John and Charles Wesley always said in their hymns, and rightly. It's also creation. Creation is grace – something we recognize every time we say "grace" before meals. It's pure gift.

'Now sin, as you all know, is ungracious behaviour. It's behaviour which rejects God's gift. We can do that in our personal lives, but we can do it in relation to creation as well. If we sit down and bolt our food, and just fill our stomachs, that is ungracious behaviour. It is a failure to recognize God's gift. That's why, as Christians, we say "grace" before meals. Even more ungracious is to return a gift and say "No thank you," or to destroy it, or to use it against others, or to poison it, or harm it. But that's what we're doing with the world God has gifted us. And that is sin, and we need salvation from that sin.

'Now I know what you'll be thinking. "Here goes Stephen with his 'green agenda'." But not at all. More than a thousand years ago in this country the Celtic church recognized that creation and redemption were completely interwoven. That's why the Celtic cross has a cross within the circle: the circle stands for the redemption of the whole of creation, not just of us humans.

'What does redemption mean in this context? Well, it means, as it always does, repentance. We have to repent and turn from our evil ways. First comes repentance, and for that we need the grace of God which the Wesleys speak of – the power of God which meets us through his Word and sacrament. But the sign of that reality is amendment of life, and in this case that means adopting different, life-affirming practices, not just in relation to our neighbours, and to God, but in relation to creation as a whole. Yes, we can sin against woods, and fields, and forests, and the animals, and in doing so we sin against God! And at harvest time God calls us not just to celebrate and to give thanks. He does call us to do that, and we are doing that, and will continue that in our Harvest Supper. He also calls us to repentance. And dare I say, and I'm speaking not as a Green Councillor but as a minister here, that does involve us in the environmental movement, in fighting for the healing of the environment just the same as we fight for human rights or for eliminating Third World debt.

The harvest supper in the Village Hall, which followed the ecumenical service, was a splendid occasion. The mood was not at all dimmed by Stephen's call to repentance. And even though a Methodist presided various forms of alcoholic refreshment flowed freely. At Rebecca and Tom's table conversation eventually got around to the theme of the sermon.

'Old Stephen's blowing his green trumpet again.'

'Well I think he's right to do so. They've been taking that theme up in *The Archers*. It's all been about GM crops recently.'

'I don't follow *The Archers*, but I'm not sure he's right. You can't really sin against creation, can you? Only against God and your neighbour.'

'Of course you can. If you mess up creation you affect God and your neighbour.'

'Yes, and I liked what he said about grace. I wondered what he was on about choosing that text, but it made sense to me.'

'Well, you all know I'm an agnostic,' said Tom, 'and "sin" has never been one of my favourite words. But if it means anything it seems to me to mean what Stephen said it did.

Unless we pay attention to what he and those like him are saying we're not going to have an earth to give thanks for.'

'Hear hear!' said Rebecca. 'And another good point we could take from his sermon is saying grace before meals. I think we should. It's a sign of gracious living. How about it?'

Questions for discussion

1. Is Stephen right, and does salvation also extend to creation? If so, what should we do about it?

2. What do we mean by 'grace', and what part does it play in salvation?

3. We talk about God as both Creator and Redeemer. How are these descriptions, or activities, of God related?

Part 2

Thinking Through The Issues

11

From What Do We Need To Be Saved?

Talk about salvation implies something we need to be saved *from*. Different cultures, religions and philosophies have identified the central problems of human life very differently.

Some religions, for example, have concentrated on *suffering*, and in the Bible the Book of Job raises this question very powerfully. Suffering can come to us in many different ways. We can think of the physical suffering associated with illness; we can think of great natural disasters like earthquakes and volcanic eruptions; we can think of events of systematic human wickedness like the Holocaust; or we can think of the mental pain of bereavement or other forms of loss. Obviously 'salvation' will be different in each case. Different human traditions also respond differently. The biblical tradition seeks healing, but others have thought that what is important is just to acknowledge that life is hard, and to rise above it, to cultivate an inner detachment, an inner freedom from the things which hurt us.

For many people *fate* is the principal enemy. For the Hindu *karma*, the entail of good or bad deeds in previous lives, determines your lot in this. It cannot be challenged, but a good life led now, in whatever station, can affect one's destiny in any future existence. The devotional (*bhakti*) strain of Hinduism believes that passionate devotion to God can obtain *release from the wheel of rebirth* (*moksha*). In the many forms of classical Hinduism this release, through devotion or good works, or ascetic discipline, is what is sought. Fatalism is by no means confined to Hinduism. A great many people believe that their lives are mapped out for them, without the consolation of any belief in a final release, except through death. Some forms of Christianity imply that everything is predestined, and at various periods there have been fierce controversies around this view.

For others *ignorance* is what we need to be liberated from. Theologians influenced by Platonism, such as Augustine, believed that we never knowingly do what we see is against our own good. If we could be taught to see, therefore, we would get things right. For many of the early Christian Fathers this was their most fundamental perspective. For them *Christ was our Teacher*, giving us knowledge of the true God, a knowledge which in itself saved us. Salvation, we might say, is a matter of learning to see things rightly, discerning the good and the true from what claims to be, but is not.

In the Hebrew Bible, where the various words for 'salvation' form a very important group, people are saved from enemies, from death, from sickness, from Sheol (the shadowy form of existence after death), and from the powers of chaos.

For the Western Christian tradition, however, *sin* is the central focus of that from which we need to be saved. Christians often use the word as if its meaning is self-evident, which it certainly is not. In the Middle Ages both theologians and artists concentrated on the 'seven deadly sins' of pride, covetousness, envy, gluttony, lust, sloth and anger. If we analyse these, we can see that they are all forms of behaviour which destroy community by putting the individual in first place. In that sense they anticipate a very familiar definition of sin as 'selfishness'. Their opposites were the virtues. In both cases the focus is on character and the way in which this may be trained to respond to God or can be hardened in ways which deny God.

In the New Testament there are four central metaphors for salvation which correspond to different aspects of sin. Redemption is a metaphor from the slave market, and thinks of delivering someone from *bondage*; reconciliation is a metaphor from the world of relationships, and thinks of the overcoming of *alienation*; justification is (arguably) a metaphor from the law courts, and thinks of deliverance from *judgment*; whilst sacrifice is a cultic metaphor looking to deliverance from *guilt* or, as is sometimes said, from *impurity.*

In the mid-twentieth century existentialism thought that we needed to be delivered from *angst*, anguish, or God forsakenness. This is what the story of Jason illustrates. Circumstances conspired against Jason. He was not able to make successful relationships. This led him to feel absolutely alone and in despair. Anyone familiar with the Samaritans will know that such feelings are only too common. They are often linked, as in Jason's case, with *guilt.* Some popular self-help books imply that guilt should be dispensed with altogether. This cannot be a Christian perspective. On the contrary, guilt is part of our humanness. It is an acknowledgment of our responsibility. But guilt is only helpful when it is forgiven. It is the possibility of forgiveness which Rebecca offers to Jason, and tries to mediate by setting up a meeting with the parents of the couple who were killed in the accident.

Another way of understanding sin can be derived from the ways in which the various words translated by 'sin' are used in Scripture. In one way or another they all refer to *forms of behaviour which destroy or diminish life.* In the Christian Scriptures God is the lifegiver, and seeks life for all God's creatures. God therefore naturally opposes all forms of behaviour which bring about death. It is not an infallible test, but it is nevertheless a useful one, to ask of any particular form of behaviour, whether it makes for life or death. Sometimes the problems are not immediately obvious. In Britain, for example, we almost all shop in supermarkets. But the use of resources implied by supermarkets, involving mass transport, and therefore large roads and huge lorries, out of town sites, the need to drive, putting local shops out of business and thus making shopping difficult for the elderly or those without a car, all raise huge questions about this seemingly normal and innocuous activity.

The Scriptures depict God as wounded by and angry about human sin. Hence arises the notion of *a gulf between God and human beings* which has to be overcome. The word 'atonement' was coined by Tyndale to express exactly this. It means quite literally 'at-one-ment'. Much Western Christian theology has focussed on the need to overcome this gulf, and I will examine this idea in a number of the sections which follow. It is often said that 'sin', as opposed to wrongdoing, is a specifically theological word, that is, defined in relation to God rather than our neighbour or the rest of creation, but Jesus' story of the sheep and the goats calls this separation into question. Those who acted in that story had no idea that they were acting in relation to the 'Son of man', God's representative, but they did so all the same. Today we have realized that we have to extend this concern to the environment, the point Stephen makes in his harvest sermon.

Although 'sin' has been the central focus of that from which we need to be saved, it is important to distinguish it from *evil*. By 'evil' here we mean the great forces which suck us up and overwhelm us, which involve individual responsibility but which go far beyond it. The later Fathers of the church spoke of this force as the Devil, and found many ways to speak of Christ's defeat of the Devil. This is the idea which Bill, the American Dominican, is developing.

The century from which we have just emerged was one of unparalleled *violence*, partly because numbers were larger than ever before, but above all because the means of destruction were greater than ever before. Many have wished to say that it is violence from which we need to be saved. We could say that violence has been added to the list of sins, or prioritized in it. We could also say that the focus has come to be on humankind's potential for destruction. Any credible theology of salvation has to address this.

This list is far from exhaustive and readers will want to add their own ideas of what we need to be saved from. In what follows I explore some of the most important areas, and the way in which salvation in relation to them has been understood.

Questions for discussion

I have identified a number of things I think we need to be saved from. Are there other things you would like to add to the list? Or things you would like to take from it? What is the 'fit' between Christ and these things?

12

Shalom

It is often said that Christianity is the most materialist of all religions, in virtue of its theology of the incarnation, according to which the Word becomes flesh. This hasn't stopped it repeatedly retreating into a primarily spiritual mode, in which the soul becomes the central focus of attention, and the body is in one way or another rejected. For this reason it is important to have frequent recourse to the Hebrew Bible, which never floats off into a purely spiritual world. Salvation is always something concrete. In Exodus, it is YHWH who is credited with the deliverance from Egypt:

> I will sing to the LORD, for he has triumphed gloriously;
>   horse and rider he has thrown into the sea.
> The LORD is my strength and my might,
>   and he has become my salvation (Ex. 15.1–2).

Similarly, it is YHWH who delivers Israel from the Philistines. Gideon is ordered to reduce his band to 300 'lest Israel vaunt themselves against me, saying, "My own hand has delivered me"' (Judg. 7.2, RSV).

Health and salvation go together. A psalm in the book of Jeremiah cries:

> Heal me, O LORD, and I shall be healed;
>   save me, and I shall be saved (Jer. 17.14).

The psalms are full of prayers for salvation which embrace most life situations. Psalm 31 thinks of a distress which destroys the writer's health:

> My eye wastes away from grief,
> my soul and body also . . .
> my strength fails because of my misery,
> and my bones waste away (Ps. 31.9–10).

Like many of the psalmists he complains of attacks from personal enemies:

> I am a scorn of all my adversaries,
>   a horror to my neighbours,
> an object of dread to my acquaintances (Ps. 31.11).

But then he prays:

> But I trust in you, O LORD . . .
> Let your face shine upon your servant;
>   save me in your steadfast love (Ps. 31.14, 16).

The single most comprehensive word to express salvation in the Hebrew Bible is *shalom* (usually translated 'peace', though sometimes also 'prosperity'). Old Testament scholars make clear that salvation and *shalom* are virtually identical. *Shalom* may mean health – the point Rebecca makes to Tom in recalling the connection between the Latin word *salus* ('health') and salvation. 'Peace, peace to the far and the near,' says YHWH in Isaiah, 'and I will heal them' (Isa. 57.19).

It means, of course, peace from enemies:

> I will both lie down and sleep in peace;
>   for you alone, O LORD, make me lie down in safety'
>   (Ps. 4.8).

It goes together with life into prosperous old age. Abram is promised:

69

You shall go to your ancestors in peace (*shalom*); you shall be buried in a good old age (Gen. 15.15).

It means prosperity:

O that you had paid attention to my commandments!
Then your prosperity (*shalom*) would have been like a river, and your success like the waves of the sea (Isa. 48.18).

As this passage makes clear, *shalom* is YHWH's gift, but it follows on obedience to God's command, which is to say, that it is contingent on the pursuit of righteousness.

One of the fullest expressions of what is meant by *shalom* is to be found in Leviticus:

If you follow my statutes and keep my commandments and observe them faithfully, I will give you your rains in their season, and the land shall yield its produce, and the trees of the field shall yield their fruit. Your threshing shall overtake the vintage, and the vintage shall overtake the sowing; you shall eat your bread to the full, and live securely in your land. And I will grant peace (*shalom*) in the land, and you shall lie down, and no one shall make you afraid; I will remove dangerous animals from the land, and no sword will go through the land . . . I will look with favour upon you and make you fruitful and multiply you (Lev. 26.3–9).

This rich, concrete, material understanding of salvation is not lost in the New Testament, as is often thought. One of the most prominent features of the Gospels are the stories of healing, where Jesus shows his concern for restoring people to wholeness. The verb 'to save' (*sozo*) is frequently used in these stories. In his dispute with the Pharisees, for example, Jesus speaks of healing as salvation (Mark 3.4). The centurion implores Jesus to heal (*diasozo*) his slave. To the woman who

70

was a sinner he says, 'Your faith has saved you' (Luke 7.50). He saves the disciples when they fear they are going to be drowned (Matt. 8.25). (Paul is likewise saved from shipwreck, Acts 27.30.) When Zacchaeus announces that he has given half of his goods to the poor, and will restore fourfold anything he took fraudulently, he announces: 'Today is salvation come to this house' (Luke 19.9).

Outside the Gospels 'salvation' is a way of talking of the totality of what Christ has brought. This includes healing, as the stories in Acts make clear. For Paul, salvation means living as part of a new type of community, the Body of Christ, where tasks are shared, and the duty of mutual care is paramount (I Cor. 11–12).

This fleshly, or bodily, aspect of salvation is later crystallized in the theology of incarnation. This recognizes that it is not just souls that need salvation, because we are body-soul-spirit unities. This aspect of salvation has always been recognized by the church through its work of 'diaconate', and the setting up of hospitals, almshouses, schools and so forth to care for the poor. It has also been recognized in the ministry of healing, and in anointing with oil.

The story of Louise's breakdown raises some of these issues. In her case the mind needed healing, but Rebecca's church, like a great many churches today, recognizes the connection between prayer and all forms of healing. Healing ceremonies can be abusive, but the one described in the story, based on that of the Iona community, is certainly not. Such healing ministry represents in one dimension a continuation of Jesus' ministry, though, as the Hebrew concern for justice indicates, it cannot be divorced from questions about the wider society.

Health represents perhaps the most central aspect of wholeness or well being. Most of us can identify with the psalmist in pulling through a serious illness, the sense that life is given back to us (I remember the tremendous sense of relief and gratitude when quinine put an end to my first bout of malaria).

Shalom, therefore, represents an indispensable dimension of salvation for embodied creatures. The problems with this view were well known to the writers of the Hebrew Bible, however. 'I saw the prosperity (*shalom*) of the wicked,' says the psalmist.

> . . . they have no pain;
>   their bodies are sound and sleek.
> They are not in trouble as others are;
>   They are not plagued like other people (Ps. 73.3–5).

The contemporary form of this problem is the 'blessings' theology which interprets material prosperity as a sign of God's favour.

Liberation theology follows the biblical witness in understanding salvation as *shalom*, as the speaker from El Salvador intimated, but it also recognizes the intimate connection in the Hebrew Bible between *shalom* and righteousness, illustrated in the passages from Isaiah and Leviticus above. According to these passages, as often in the prophets, the failure of social justice makes true *shalom*, or salvation, impossible. God wills salvation as *shalom*, therefore, but for all, and not for the few at the expense of the many.

Questions for discussion

1. Do you agree that *shalom* is an essential aspect of any theology of salvation? If not, why not?

2. What is the connection between peace and righteousness, and what do we do about it?

3. Is cancelling Third World Debt part of 'salvation'? Whether you agree or disagree, how would you argue your case?

13

Sacrifice

If *shalom* is one main strand of thinking about salvation in the Hebrew Bible, sacrifice is another. For many Christians this remains the most important image for understanding the death of Christ.

Paul writes to the Christians in Corinth that 'Christ died for our sins in accordance with the scriptures' (I Cor. 15.3). Earlier he compares Jesus to the paschal lamb who is offered (I Cor. 5.7). In his letter to the Roman community he says that Jesus was 'put forward as a sacrifice of atonement (*hilasterion*) by his blood, effective through faith' (Rom. 3.25). The author of Ephesians writes that 'Christ loved us and gave himself up for us, a fragrant offering and sacrifice (*thusia*) for us' (Eph. 5.2). According to the Letter to the Hebrews Christ 'entered once for all into the Holy Place, not with the blood of goats and calves, but with his own blood, thus obtaining eternal redemption' (Heb. 9.12).

This is very powerful imagery, and has always formed part of the way people understand the significance of the cross. But what does the imagery actually say?

First, sacrifice is sometimes propitiatory, that is, designed to ward off the anger of God. In Protestant Christianity the emphasis on the 'wrath of God', and its conjunction with the death of Jesus, seemed to suggest such an understanding. The Anglican Prayer Book translated the term *hilasterion* in Romans 3.25 as 'propitiation', and this was incorporated into the Communion service, underlining such a view. Human sin provoked God's wrath, but Jesus' death took it away.

In the Hebrew Bible, though some sacrifice is clearly propitiatory, most was probably not. For example, the majority of sacrifice, as in contemporary Hinduism, probably involved no blood at all, and was a thank-offering. The thank-offering involves the surrender of a portion of one's crops, or of other food, in thanks to God for the blessings of health, security and sustenance. It has what we would today call a sacramental significance. The offering signifies the total life offering of the believer – gratitude in response to grace.

Some sacrifice which involved blood was not propitiatory. The Passover lamb was a case in point, where the lamb was butchered and then eaten by the family or community group. This is a very common form of sacrifice in South India today, and is what is called a 'communion sacrifice'. Killing an animal in a sacred context is arguably far more humane than taking it to an abattoir. When the group eat it together they affirm their fellowship. In Israel the Passover lamb recalled the escape from Egypt and thus signified freedom.

The sacrifices which are usually translated 'sin offering' (*hatta'th*), guilt offering (*'asham*) and 'whole burnt offering' (*'olam*) all had atoning significance, that is, they were all thought to overcome the breach between God and humans created by sin. They are not necessarily propitiatory, but they do presuppose that sin is so serious that the offering of life is needed to restore fellowship. Once again, the offering has sacramental significance. The death of the animal stands for the penitent life-offering of the believer. Since sacrifice occurred within the framework of the covenant, some commentators emphasize that sacrifice was a gracious provision by God to restore fellowship.

In one of the most famous passages of the Hebrew Bible the word 'guilt offering' is used of the servant of Isaiah 53. There it is said that it was:

> the will of the LORD to bruise him;
>   he has put him to grief;
> when he makes himself an offering for sin (*'asham*),
>   he shall see his offspring, he shall prolong his days;
> the will of the LORD shall prosper in his hand;

he shall see the fruit of the travail of his soul and be
    satisfied;
by his knowledge shall the righteous one, my servant,
    make many to be accounted righteous;
    and he shall bear their iniquities (Isa. 53.10, RSV).

From a very early period, if not in the New Testament itself,
(and this is arguable), this passage was understood to refer to
the death of Christ. How should we understand it?

One very common phrase used of it is that Jesus 'paid the
price of sin'. This is the language of penal retribution. If
someone commits an offence, we say that they have to 'pay'
for it, usually these days by a prison term, though in Britain
until the 1960s, and still in many countries, some crimes are
'paid for' by death. As this thinking applies to the death of
Christ, the argument goes like this: God is holy, and therefore
cannot brook sin. God cannot overlook it without compromising God's righteousness. God may be merciful, but sin cannot
simply be forgiven by fiat. Sin is costly; it deserves death. In
order then, both to pay the price for sin, and not to compromise
God's holiness, God sends God's Son to die in our place.

Since at least the sixteenth century there have been those who
have argued that this implies an unworthy picture of God. By
and large we mostly do not demand death for offences
committed against us. Pictures of those in favour of the death
penalty in the United States dancing around prisons with
posters saying, 'Fry, baby fry', as a murderer is executed,
properly awake revulsion. Surely God does not behave like
this? Why must there be *death* for sin to be forgiven?

In the twelfth century Anselm wrote the first full-scale
treatise on the atonement under the heading, *Why did God
become man?* The category he used was that of 'satisfaction',
which is not identical with that of sacrifice, but contains a
significant overlap. The language of satisfaction is also that of
penal retribution. In the world of his day, any offence

demanded 'satisfaction' (until well into the nineteenth century 'gentlemen' might demand 'satisfaction' for an offence, which often took the form of a duel). Satisfaction was graded depending on your status in society. The same offence committed against a peasant, a knight, a lord, and the King, would trigger quite different penalties. But what, Anselm asked, about offences against God? God was infinite, and therefore, logically, even the smallest offence against God was infinite. Since all of us commit offences, how on earth could we make satisfaction for them? And that was precisely the point: on earth we certainly could not. What was needed was a 'God-man', in solidarity with us, and therefore able to represent us as sinners, but also true God, and therefore in a position to make satisfaction for an infinite offence.

Anselm explains the need to make satisfaction by resort to a metaphor which remains important in legal discussion to this day: that of balance. Anselm writes his theology very much as this series has been envisaged, in the form of a dialogue. His interlocutor, Boso, was a real person, probably a pupil, and the dialogue may express the contents of a real tutorial (as some of the conversations of my story have their origin in real life). Boso objects that trivial sins can be passed over. Anselm replies: 'You have not yet weighed the seriousness of sin.' In other words, bleeding heart liberals have got it wrong. The universe is an intensely serious moral place. To pretend otherwise is to throw the moral balance of reality out of kilter. Sin does that, and Christ's satisfaction restores it. In recent times some legal theorists have argued that crime can be understood as the law-breaking taking advantage of the law-abiding. Punishment restores the balance.

John Stott, an advocate of such views, protests against caricatures:

There is nothing even remotely immoral here, since the substitute for the lawbreakers is none other than the divine

Lawgiver himself . . . the righteous, loving Father humbled himself to become in and through his only Son flesh, sin and a curse for us, in order to redeem us without compromising his own character.[1]

For Christ not to die is to compromise God's righteousness, God's hatred of sin. But this view does not answer the questions raised by the very nature of punishment. The difficulty for Christians is that *forgiveness* indisputably lies at the heart of the gospel. How do forgiveness and punishment go together? These issues are explored in the first story. Do we forgive only when someone has 'paid the price' for their wrongdoing? That does not seem to be the implication of Jesus' teaching that we must forgive 'until seventy times seven' times when someone offends us. Many arguments in favour of punishment seem to suggest that forgiveness is letting someone off the hook, an easy option. On the contrary, it is a remorselessly difficult practice, a craft that may take a lifetime to learn. The suggestion of the Gospels is that it might be forgiveness rather than punishment that enables 'repentance and amendment of life'.

The logic of paying the price and of satisfaction also need tough scrutiny. As George Bernard Shaw pointed out, the logic of the first seems to be that two wrongs make a right: that if you do something terrible to me, we are quits if I do something equally terrible to you. This axiom, a form of the balance argument, cannot be the gospel. As the gentleman's 'I demand satisfaction' suggests, the premise of satisfaction is honour, which is indeed the background to Anselm's argument. But must Christ die for God's honour? Or ours? Or that of the universe? Why, precisely, is satisfaction demanded for an offence? To the objection that sin cannot be ignored, we have to insist that forgiveness is not ignoring it. Is, then, Christ's

---

[1] John Stott, *The Cross of Christ*, IVP 1989, p. 168.

death a sign of the costliness of forgiveness to God? I think that in some sense it is, but this is different either from 'paying the price', or dying as a 'sacrifice for sin'.

Raymond Schwager has turned the traditional understanding of atonement by sacrifice on its head. He argues that the need for Christ's death was not to reconcile God to us, because of the barrier created by our sin with an all holy God, but to reconcile us to God, to remove our hatred of the Good. We have convinced ourselves that we cannot be acceptable to God and we keep ourselves at a distance. We imprison ourselves. The force of the announcement that Jesus 'bore our sins in his body on the cross' (I Peter 2.24, NRSV) is that God needs no reparation but leaves the door open for us, waiting for us to turn from our own hatred. We are like the Police Chief, Javer, in Victor Hugo's *Les Misérables,* whom Tom mentions. We are comfortable with the world of stern judgment. We seek it. And when we find that what is there is not judgment but forgiveness, we do not know what to make of it.

Questions for discussion

1. What is the relationship between the death of Jesus and forgiveness?

2. In the West we no longer literally sacrifice animals or vegetable offerings. 'Sacrifice', however, is still a very rich and loaded word. What are its dimensions?

3. How do you 'pay the price' for any crime or sin?

14

The Scapegoat

When people feel guilty they frequently deal with their guilt by displacement. They project their guilt on another person or group who then becomes 'guilty of everything'. This is the scapegoat mechanism. Scapegoating has played a major role in human history, and remains a destructive force in all forms of community, including families. The history of the Jews in Europe between the tenth century and the twentieth can largely be understood in terms of scapegoating. When things went wrong, whether through famine or plague or as a result of economic forces, a scapegoat was sought, and the Jews, who would not toe the dominant Christian line, were a convenient target. So began the history of pogroms and expulsions which culminated in the Holocaust. The antisemitic literature used by the Nazis was classic scapegoating literature, blaming Germany's ills on a world-wide Zionist conspiracy. The scapegoat mechanism can be seen at work in almost all communities in conflict. Some psychologists suggest that every family and community has its own scapegoat.

The idea of the scapegoat is not properly a theory of sacrifice, but it has strong analogies with it. An account of the scapegoat ritual is found in Leviticus 16 alongside an account of a sin offering in which a bull and a goat are slaughtered. As such it is put on all fours as a provision made by God for removing sin. The passage from Isaiah 53 mentioned in the last section speaks of the Servant 'bearing the sins' of others. This is the language of the scapegoat. In the ritual the priest lays both his hands on the head of the live goat and confesses over it 'all the iniquities of the people of Israel, and all their transgressions, all their sins, putting them on the head of the goat, and sending it away into the wilderness by means of someone designated for the task. The goat shall bear on itself all their iniquities to a barren region; and the goat shall be set free in the wilderness'(Lev. 16 21–22).

The similarities between the idea of the scapegoat bearing away sin and the Servant doing so make it unsurprising that Christ has been understood as the divine scapegoat, taking our sins upon him, and bearing them away. In society at large, however, the displacement activity of scapegoating is anything but redemptive. Can we appropriate it for Christ?

The cultural anthropologist René Girard has made the scapegoat the central focus of his work. Girard believes that primitive societies were characterized by 'the war of all against all'. This was prompted by the fundamental human attribute of *mimesis* ('imitation'). We learn by *mimesis*, and we adopt role models whom we both respect and fear. The model calls us to imitation, but if we imitate it completely, then we displace it. We are, as Girard has it, quoting Hamlet, 'to double business bound'.

This double bind leads to violence. The answer to this violence, in Girard's view, was the scapegoat mechanism. On his account of it, some individual would be chosen, perhaps the priest-king, who would be ritually killed by the whole community once a year. Stoning, which is a punishment prescribed for a number of offences in the Hebrew Bible, was a way of killing an offender which ensured that the whole community bore the guilt. Were there to be second thoughts, no one could turn round and say: 'It was nothing to do with me.' On Girard's theory, all the pent-up violence and aggression of the community would be expended on the victim, and thus the scapegoat really did deliver the community from self-destruction for a time. As aggression once again built up, so another scapegoat would be sought. The religious dimension of scapegoating is essential for Girard, for on his theory religion is what conceals from us the reality of violence, and indeed, in a way, even sanctifies it. He makes no distinction between the scapegoat and sacrifice. For him all theologies of sacrifice are rationalizations of violence. We cannot face up to our violence, so we rationalize it in sacrificial theories and argue that it is divinely commanded. But the 'divine' here is nothing but what society as a whole demands, as the French sociologist Durkheim argued.

From this anthropological base Girard turns to the Gospels, to the passage in which Christ says that he will reveal things 'hidden from the foundation of the world' (Matt. 13.35). This, says Girard, is the secret of violence, the scapegoat mechanism. Christ himself dies as a scapegoat, but in doing so exposes the myth of violence, and thereby opens the way to a society founded on a love which refuses violence. Girard argues that in the Gospels we have a revelation which presents a critique of all religion (which is all bound up with the sanctification of violence).

Girard's views have been widely canvassed by theologians, even though it works on the level of unprovable grand theory. In pointing to the connections between religion, sacrifice and violence he seems to have uncovered something very profound, to some extent evidenced by the violence of religions with a sacrificial agenda and rhetoric. Given Christianity's long history of violence against heretics, Jews, witches and subordinated populations, and given the universal agreement that forgiveness and non-violence was at the heart of Jesus' preaching of the kingdom, his arguments deserve reflection.

Questions for discussion

1. What does it mean to say that Christ 'bears our sins'? In what way is this redemptive?

2. How does scapegoating operate in the communities you know?

3. What is it that Christ reveals, and can it be said to save us?

15

Example

At the opposite extreme from the grim realities of scapegoating, and to some extent scenting the violence implied in sacrifice, is the theme of learning by love, or example. The biblical root of this view is the undoubted importance of Jesus' life and teaching. The Gospels are not just stories about Jesus' death. They tell us very significant things about what he did and said, from which Christians have always wanted to learn. Developing this side of the gospel story, some theologians have argued that the way in which Christ saves us is by evoking a response of love from us. This has been dubbed the 'exemplary' or 'moral influence' theory of the atonement, and was widely canvassed at the beginning of the twentieth century.

By the end of the twentieth century this theory had been widely dismissed as inadequate to the reality of the trenches and the death camps. It smacks of headmasterly exhortations to do better or try harder, and seems not to take account of the reality of tragedy and evil. Can it be defended?

We need to say straight away that this 'theory' has often been misrepresented. Those who have taught it have usually insisted on the saving power of grace in our lives. Grace here is understood, as it has been for so much of the Christian tradition, as a power God communicates to us, which we may appropriate or refuse, and which works in us for amendment of life. A way of thinking of this with which we are more comfortable today is to think of the ceaseless operation of God's Spirit working for life, and against death, for good and against evil. John tells us that the Spirit will 'make Christ known', which we understand to mean that Christ is not just a historical figure, though he is also that, but also a present reality 'in our midst'. How are we to understand that? As the church has always insisted from St Paul onwards, God's Spirit can speak to us through the Scriptures, which includes, of course, the narrative of the Gospels. In the Middle Ages there developed the notion of 'the imitation of Christ', and this, like Ignatius Loyola's later Exercises, works by imaginative appropriation of the Gospel stories into our own lives. 'Example', then, is a very pallid way of talking of what is going on here. Rather, meditation on the Gospel story saturates our life, a bit like tanning a skin. We appropriate it so deeply that it becomes part of us, and thus determines how we act towards others. This is not 'works righteousness' because it is understood that it is God's Spirit which 'opens up' the Scriptures to us, and enables us to hear them in the first place.

Another way in which this has been envisaged is to think of the unbroken chain of disciples, from Peter, James and John till our own day, each handing on the torch of their new and redeemed selfhood to the next generation. When the feminist theologian Rosemary Ruether writes that those who have been liberated can in turn become liberating persons for others, she is not far from this view.

Whichever way we understand it, we see that it is impossible to think of Calvary without Pentecost. We sing, 'Once only, once, and once for all / His precious life he gave,' but in fact God's work in history is ceaseless, making the effects of the cross real in every generation. As Bill puts it in the story, redemption is a process. There may or may not be a critical moment in our lives which we identify as the moment of conversion, but life does not stop there. For each person, and for history as a whole, salvation can only be understood as an ongoing process.

This approach to salvation has obvious echoes of the Patristic idea of Christ as our Teacher, and therefore of life as a process of education. This, too, necessarily understands Christ and the Spirit together, for it is the Spirit who makes Christ known. But does it meet the challenge of evil and tragedy? Once again the penal situation can help us. The great Anglican theologian Robert Moberly argued that punishment which did not set out to be rehabilitative was immoral. But how are people rehabilitated? Part of the answer must be in terms of education, understood in the broadest sense. Of course a clever person can use skills and knowledge for wicked purposes, but education is more than the acquisition of knowledge and skills: it has an inescapably moral dimension. To use the Jesuit term, all education is about formation. Human history, then, could be understood as formation under the pedagogy of the Spirit.

In the face of the appalling crimes of the twentieth century we have become sceptical of both progress and the civilizing power of culture. It was the nation which regarded itself as having a cultural mission to the rest of the world which gave its support to Hitler. Ought we not to be wary of the very idea of education? Once again I think that the answer is 'No'. The Brazilian educationalist Paulo Freire entitled his great work on adult education, *The Pedagogy of the Oppressed* (Penguin 1972). Beginning from teaching people basic literacy, he understood education as a process of conscientization. People who had been conditioned for centuries to think of themselves as nothing but poor and ignorant, deserving of nothing, were taught to see that this was a very convenient doctrine for those in power, and then to take responsibility for their own struggles for freedom. Works righteousness! No, why should we call it that? If we read Isaiah, then surely the Pedagogy of the Spirit is precisely the pedagogy of the oppressed, continuing the 'Nazareth manifesto' into the present.

Questions for discussion

1. How important is example in the shaping of our lives?

2. What does the 'imitation of Christ' involve?

3. If salvation involves liberation in some way, what are its dimensions?

16

The Crucified God

Gautama (the Buddha) thought that suffering was the central problem which human beings had to face. He had in mind chiefly 'the manifold ills which flesh is heir to'. This dimension of experience is usually thought of in connection with the so-called 'problem of evil'. Under that heading one section is usually devoted to moral evil. The scale of atrocities in the twentieth century, however, produced another response, already anticipated a century earlier by the Russian novelist Dostoevsky. The sacrificial view of the atonement concentrates on human sin, and asks, 'How can it be atoned for?' In the light of the scale of human evil manifest in two world wars, the Holocaust, Hiroshima, Vietnam, people asked, 'How can we believe in a good God? If there is a supreme being, is he not a devil?' On this view, it is not humans who are in the dock, but God. To the extent that we are looking at humans, we are concentrating not on the suffering which is part of the human lot, but on the terror of history. Amongst others, the German theologian Jürgen Moltmann has tried to address the question these events raise. Adrian's Good Friday reflections, which Rebecca recalls when she and Tom are discussing Josef's story, are based on Moltmann's book *The Crucified God*.

Moltmann begins by dismissing the tradition of theodicy – the attempt to 'justify the ways of God to man'. In the face of the Holocaust, he says, such an attempt becomes almost blasphemous. But are we then reduced to silence? His attempt to fashion an answer leads to the theology of the crucified God. At the centre of his great exposition lies the story from Elie Wiesel's *Night*, which Rebecca struggles to recall. Wiesel, who was in Auschwitz (like Josef, a real person whose details I have altered), tells the story of three people who were hanged in front of the camp inmates for some offence or other. One of them was a boy, and he struggled for life at the end of the rope.

Watching this, someone said, 'Where is God?' As his struggles went on, the question was repeated. And then, Wiesel says, came the answer: 'He is there, hanging on the gallows.'

Reflecting on this story Moltmann tries to understand it in a trinitarian way. Christ, who also died on a gallows, expresses the divine solidarity with all the victims of history. Note that here it is not so much divine anger at human wrong which is being expressed, as in the sacrificial view. It is rather the divine response to the human accusation of the absence of God in the face of terror. In the background is Dostoevsky's *The Brothers Karamazov*, and the atheist Ivan's indignant claim that in the face of human cruelty he would return his ticket to the world. The focus is not on the perpetrator but the victim.

But what is salvific about God's identification with the victim? This question partly lay behind the classical rejection of the idea that God could suffer. If two people are both in the same pit, neither can help the other out. If God is as helpless as human beings, what hope have we? Moltmann's answer to this problem has two stages. First, he insists that if God is to love, then God must know what it is to suffer. A God who cannot suffer cannot be involved, and cannot love either. Further, God's 'omnipotence' cannot exclude the possibility of powerlessness, for a merely omnipotent being would only be feared and not loved.

More profoundly, he explores the idea (not original to him) that the cross is the key to our understanding of the Trinity. 'Anyone who really talks of the Trinity talks of the cross of Jesus, and does not speculate in heavenly riddles.'[1] On the cross God the Son suffers dying, but God the Father is not 'absent' from the event, but 'suffers the death of the Son' in the grief of love. What 'proceeds' from the event of the death of the Son and the Father's loss is the Spirit which justifies the godless and raises the dead. On the cross, 'the whole uproar of

---

[1] Jürgen Moltmann, *The Crucified God*, SCM Press 1974, p. 207.

history' is taken up into God. As Rebecca tries to explain, this is salvific because it puts events which are sheer wickedness, expressions of unmeaning, in the context of the divine life, and thus holds out the hope of vindication in the future. To use Moltmann's own words, 'There is no suffering which in this history of God is not God's suffering; no death which has not been God's death in the history of Golgotha. Therefore there is no life, no fortune and no joy which have not been integrated by his history into eternal life, into the eternal joy of God.'[2]

Tom objects to Rebecca's arguments that it seems like 'pie in the sky' to him. But the point about pie in the sky was to teach people not to worry about what was going on here on earth. Hope for the victim, by contrast, rests on the resurrection of Jesus, and the risen Jesus bears the marks of the nails and the spear-thrust – in other words, the resurrection is in continuity with what happens here. It is a new creation, but it also belongs to the whole of life. Far from being a reason for a life without protest, it is, on the contrary, reason for full acceptance of life here, and a life lived in struggle and hope.

It is important to distinguish this account of redemption from the patristic and mediaeval idea of Christ as a Victim. The first stanza of 'Sing, my tongue, the glorious battle' ends:

> Tell how Christ, the world's Redeemer,
> As a Victim won the day.

Victimhood here was Christ's willing assumption of sacrifice. This theology evoked a mysticism of suffering which understood pain as something positive, an identification with the crucified Christ. The theology of the crucified God, by contrast, looks to a future state of *shalom*. It seeks peace and justice now, seeking the conversion of the persecutor, the godforsaken and dehumanized who man the systems of terror,

---

2 Ibid., p. 246.

but also hopes for the vindication of the victim in the new creation. To use the technical language of theology, it is eschatological, a hope for the 'last days', which also acts powerfully here and now. The cross, then, has been taken from the isolation of the sacrificial theory, and understood as lying at the heart of the ongoing life of the Triune God, open to history, open to vulnerability, actively seeking the salvation of the godless and godforsaken.

Questions for discussion

1. Moltmann argues that it is impossible to think about salvation without a doctrine of the Trinity. What do you think?

2. If salvation is 'eschatological', to do with the 'last' things, does that mean that nothing happens in this life?

3. How does the suffering of God help us, if at all?

17

The Powers

In his intervention at the meeting on El Salvador, Bill, the Dominican, introduces the idea of 'the powers'. The idea of the powers is prominent in the Hebrew Bible. Psalm 74 speaks of God crushing the powers of chaos:

> Yet God my King is from of old,
>   working salvation in the earth.
> You divided the sea by your might;
>   you broke the heads of the dragons in the waters.
> You crushed the heads of Leviathan;
>   you gave him as food for the creatures of the wilderness
> (Ps. 74.12–14).

In these verses, the 'sea', the 'dragons' and Leviathan are all symbols of primaeval chaos which God subdues.

The Book of Daniel speaks of a conflict between the angels of God and the angels of Persia and Greece (Dan. 10). The author (or authors) of Colossians and Ephesians talk of principalities and powers which are in recognizable continuity with these forces. In Colossians Christ is spoken of as 'disarming' the principalities and powers, 'making a public example of them' and thereby triumphing over them (Col. 2.15).

This language appealed to many of the Church Fathers, who elaborated it, often in a grotesque way. Some thought of Christ defeating Satan, some as deceiving him, some as a bait to trap him, some as a ransom paid to him. Later, it was argued that such ideas were immoral, as Satan had no rights. Though Luther used this imagery to great effect at the Reformation, it tended to be by-passed in the centuries which followed, and in the nineteenth century positively forgotten. At the end of the First World War the Swedish bishop Gustav Aulen resurrected it, and dubbed it the 'Classic' theory of the atonement. It made an impact because this mythical language spoke only too clearly to the highly mythicized regimes of Fascism and Stalinism, and was taken up and used by many theologians. It is, however, the American theologian Walter Wink who has above all made them the subject of theological reflection in his magnificent trilogy on this theme. I have put some of his views into Bill's mouth, and in what follows I am summarizing the argument of his second volume, *Engaging the Powers*.

When we discuss the powers, we are reflecting about that dimension of evil, far transcending the ability of any individual to counter, from which human beings need to be saved. Wink speaks of the powers as the 'interiority' of movements, cultures, nations, churches, and movements. This does not mean that the powers are not objective entities. They may very well be. In terms of our experience, however, what is important is that there is no way we can escape their influence. As the spiritualities of movements and cultures, they shape our lives to their deepest depths. Thus the spirituality of nationalism was a 'power' responsible for many of the bloodiest conflicts of the twentieth century.

Wink identifies violence as the true spirituality of our day. He shows by an analysis of popular comic strips and TV programmes how we are conditioned to assume that violence is the answer to all our problems. We all know the thrill when, at the end of an hour or two, the good guy, bleeding and battered, finally gets the better of the bad guy. Justice is done! (Henry Fonda's *High Noon* is a good example.) What is going on here, says Wink, is that we identify with the good guy but project our own repressed anger, violence or lust on the bad guy. For the majority of the film in which the bad guy is winning, we can vicariously enjoy our own dark side, but in the closing minutes we reassert control over it. Salvation comes through identification with the hero, and indeed the good/evil motif is often very clearly highlighted, as in the Superman comics. But we do not have to go to comic strips for this. It is only too clearly what is going on in *Paradise Lost*, and the reason why there is so much less energy in *Paradise Regained*! Wink points out that the theme is extremely ancient, as the motif is basically there in the Babylonian creation myths, and we have an echo of it in the passage from Psalm 74 quoted above. What emerges from this dualistic way of looking at the world he calls the 'domination system', because human affairs can be mapped by the struggle for domination. With many feminists he believes that there was a time before the domination system ('pre-fall') but the system has been with us since the dawn of recorded history. Patriarchy is a central aspect of it. Israel was not exempt from the domination system: exhortations to holy war, and the use of the death penalty for the mildest sexual indiscretions, are examples of this. But in prophetic preaching, and in the life and teaching of Jesus, we find an outline of God's domination-free order. The New Testament words *kosmos* ('world'), *aeon* ('age') and *sarx* ('flesh') are various ways of speaking of the domination system. They represent society organized against God, operating according to assumptions which are contrary to God. For this reason they become the focus of God's wrath and redemptive activity. In Wink's terms, the powers are good, fallen, and can be redeemed.

That the powers are good follows from Colossians 1.16–17: 'For in him all things in heaven and on earth were created, things visible and invisible, whether thrones or dominions or rulers or powers – all things have been created through him and for him. He himself is before all things, and in him all things hold together.'

In the preceding verse the author says that we are redeemed from the world of darkness, which is the world of the powers, so how can God have created them? What these powers represent, says Wink, are the institutional structures without which we cannot exist. Only through institutions can ideas be put into action, but the powers 'fall' when from being penultimate they become ultimate, and, like the Arena Government in El Salvador, arrogate the divine prerogative of dispensing life and death.

In Romans Paul famously tells that the powers that be are ordained of God. This means that they are necessary to support life. But God at the same time condemns the system to the extent that it obstructs the realization of *shalom*, peace and justice, and presses for its transformation into a more human system. What Jesus calls the kingdom is not a vision of the world destroyed but of the world transformed. Redemption, as Wink sets it out, means first of all a liberating forgiveness for our own sin and for complicity with the powers, and then engagement in liberating the powers from their bondage to idolatry.

The first step in this process is unmasking the 'delusional assumptions' of the domination system. Virtually everywhere the powers clothe themselves as angels of light: like the Arena government they speak the language of freedom, justice and democracy. Throughout the world there are thousands of people who have tortured others, and did so with a good conscience. Many Latin American torturers continued to go to Mass every day. They were not sadists, Wink comments. They had surrendered themselves to the idol of the state, and this action changed the definitions of good and evil on which they operated. What served the state was good, what opposed it was evil. Torture was a means of opposing evil. No doubt this was true for many of the tens of thousands who staffed the Nazi death camps, as for those involved in ethnic cleansing in Serbia and Bosnia.

Opposed to the domination system is God's domination-free order, which is a world characterized by equality, holiness, the breaking down of ethnic and racial divisions, equality between the sexes, and thus the end of patriarchy, and non-violence. It is the cross, when it breaks the spiral of violence, which inaugurates this order. Jesus took upon himself the violence of the ruling system of the day, and refused to return it: 'When he was abused, he did not return abuse; when he suffered, he did not threaten; but he trusted himself to the one who judges justly' (I Peter 2.23). Jesus' death did not confirm the legitimacy of Roman power, but on the contrary called it into question, de-absolutized it.

How does this work out in the life of the believer? Jesus spoke of losing one's life to save it. Paul speaks of dying to sin. Wink translates Colossians 2.20: 'If with Christ you died to the fundamental assumptions of the Domination system (the customary rules and regulations by which society is governed) why do you let yourselves be dictated to as if your lives were still controlled by that System.' We need to die, Wink argues, to our love of bondage to our various idolatries. This is a dying to the domination system in all its manifestations. It goes beyond 'personal conversion' because it recognizes that who we are as people is shaped by the systems in which we live. The powers represent the social bonds within which we are trapped. Many South African evangelicals died to their privatized egos, Wink remarks, but not to apartheid, and we can multiply examples around the world. When we die to our idolatries we delegitimate an unjust system and create a spiritual counter-climate.

Amongst the delusional assumptions of our society Wink lists the following:

Money is the most important value.

The possession of money is a sign of worth.

The production of material goods is more important than the production of healthy and normal people.

Property is sacred and property ownership is an absolute right.[1]

---

[1] Walter Wink, *Engaging the Powers*, Fortress Press 1992, p. 95.

If Wink is right about this, and I believe he is, then perhaps we need to qualify his judgment that violence is the spirituality of our age. Put variously money, growth, and material possessions are at the heart of our spirituality. This involves violence, of course, because, if we do not have them, we may need to use violence to get them, and if we have them, we need to defend them. By violence here I do not mean the use of handguns: I am talking about corporate 'downsizing', predatory take-overs, the need for competition. In these ways violence and the centrality of money go together. Together they constitute the ethos, the interiority of capitalism, which is the ruling power of our age. In Wink's terms capitalism, and structures like those of the World Bank, the IMF and the WTO, are good, fallen, and need redemption. They are good in that we need mechanisms by which people can be clothed, housed and fed, and by which human ingenuity can be channelled for the common good. They are fallen in that they are used for the profit of the few, 'and the Devil take the hindmost'.

What would their redemption mean? Jesus frequently spoke of the need to renounce possessions. This does not mean, I think, that we all have to live like St Francis, but it does mean that possessions exist, as the early church recognized, for the common good, and not for private gain. Changing this requires changing our spirituality, which is what would concretely make for salvation today.

Questions for discussion

1. How would you identify the powers from which we need to be saved?

2. How exactly does Christ overcome the powers?

3. What is our part as persons in the overcoming of evil?

18

No Other Name?

'There is salvation in no one else,' says Peter, in his speech to the Jewish authorities, 'for there is no other name under heaven given among mortals by which we must be saved' (Acts 4.12). This is a quotation often found on the lips of Christians who go to churches like St Michael's. It is usually taken to imply that those who do not 'confess Christ as Lord' are not destined for eternal salvation (this is often put in the less friendly form of being destined for hell). This is explained with regret, and a questioning shrug of the shoulders, but 'that's the way it is'. This is how God has ordained it.

This approach to salvation has a very long pedigree. Cyprian of Carthage, in the third century, was the first to announce that there was 'no salvation outside the church'. This was not primarily directed at the pagan world, but at heretics, backsliders and schismatics. It was a way of keeping people in line. Augustine was convinced that baptism was the gateway to eternal life. Unbaptized infants, he said, will suffer *mitissima damnatio* – the mildest form of damnation. In this view he was followed by both Catholic and Protestant orthodoxy. These views were challenged at least as early as the sixteenth century and increasingly from the eighteenth century on. In the twentieth century there was a stand-off between self-styled 'biblical Christians', holding to the traditional view, and those who could not agree with them, contemptuously styled 'liberals'. 'The Human Touch' story is meant to explore some of the issues in the debate.

Very often the debate is couched between religions. There are self-evidently holy people in other religious traditions. Can we write off the traditions which produce them? This is to conceive the problem too narrowly. The contemporary world, like Augustine's fourth- and fifth-century world, is full of people like Tom, who are morally serious, 'full of good works', often contribute far more to the causes of social justice than their Christian peers, but who are not believers. What about good pagans, asked Augustine's contemporaries? 'The best works of good pagans are nothing but splendid vices,' he replied, on the grounds that only grace produces truly good works, and grace only comes with believing.

There are two questions about this type of view. First, does it really represent the God we find in Jesus, the God witnessed to by the Scriptures as a whole? Could the God whose nature was love, which is to say mercy and righteousness, consign the vast majority of human beings who have ever lived to eternal damnation without blinking? Were a human judge to act in this way, he would be deluged by petitions from Anmesty International, which is supported, in my experience of Amnesty groups, largely by people like Tom. That great numbers of otherwise well-meaning Christians are prepared to affirm this suggests to me that the 'God' being spoken of is the projection of their shadow. It also seems to me to illustrate the way in which Scripture can function as a fetish. A fetish is a human construct which demands human blood, which dehumanizes its devotees.

All religions have many examples in their history of dehumanizing forms of behaviour, and Christianity is no exception. Its record, in fact, may be rather worse than that of others. The language of hell and damnation is the language of violence and destruction, and quite often the language of hatred ('Go to hell!') We are reminded of Girard's thesis that religious language has served to rationalize violence against the other. What behaviour follows, we have to ask ourselves, from belief which is prepared to damn most of one's fellow creatures? The answer we are given is that we must redouble efforts at evangelization. But there is also the historical record to inspect. The song writer Leon Rosselson, in his powerful 'Stand Up for Judas', writes: 'Two thousand cruel years have shown the way that Jesus led.' Since no reading of the Sermon on the Mount can make Jesus a prophet of violence, we are back with Girard again.

The second problem is that these views of salvation seem to imply a very parochial form of God. Does God confine God's activity only to Israel and church? (And only to certain forms of the church at that: not the Protestants, according to the Counter Reformation, and *vice versa*; and not the liberals, according to St Michael's.) On the evidence of the Scriptures this is a very implausible view. God calls all things into being, according to Genesis, bringing order out of chaos. God's Spirit is abroad, active and fashioning, then, in all of reality. God has a special destiny for Israel, certainly, but works through all of the nations. Isaiah looks forward to the day when 'Israel will be the third with Egypt and Assyria, a blessing in the midst of the earth, whom the LORD of hosts has blessed, saying "Blessed be Egypt my people, and Assyria the work of my hands, and Israel my heritage"' (Isa. 19.24–25). For Egypt and Assyria we can substitute all the nations and cultures of the earth.

In the eighteenth century the Lutheran theologian and philosopher, J. G. Herder, suggested that God's Spirit expresses its richness in the diversity of all human cultures. In his passion for Rembrandt and Shakespeare, Tom is expressing something like this view. We need to go back to salvation as *shalom*. *Shalom* is peace and justice, but it is also more than that. It is the struggle for life and the expression of life, which honours the God of life. Karl Barth famously found a witness to God's providence in the music of Mozart, even though the composer was not an especially pious individual. In the same way we can understand all that is life-giving as a striving towards the God of life, rather as a plant strives up towards the sun. It is natural to turn to the great artists, writers and composers as examples of this. We do not understand the mystery of human genius, but it is certain that in each generation a few individuals are able to express what the vast majority of us can only guess at. However, I have put it more generally, because the humblest human activities can represent that striving towards the sun, and can be profound expressions of grace. Following Herder we can think of God's Spirit ceaselessly active in the whole of both creation and history, and, like God's Word, its operations are not in vain (Isa. 55.11).

Salvation – healing, wholeness, well being – follows from the touch of the living God. As Tom, the agnostic, was struggling to express it, the reality of salvation can be found in many 'non-religious' contexts (if God is the Creator of all things, is there such a thing?). This does not mean that Rebecca is wrong to go to church, or that there is no point in believing. It does mean that the point of believing is not to obtain an entrance ticket to heaven. Believing, as the saints and mystics have always put it, is much more like being in love: its reward is the joy of an ever deepening relationship with God. This can spill over and engage others, as Rebecca's faith seems to do with Tom (though we don't know the end of the story). At the same time, believers always have much to learn from unbelievers (a point Karl Barth always insisted on), whose antennae for the realities of salvation, places where the living God breaks through, albeit unrecognized, may well be much more sensitive than those of believers.

Questions for discussion

1. How important is religion, and in particular Christianity, in any understanding of salvation?

2. What are we to make of passages in the New Testament, like Matthew 23, for example, which depict hell for the wicked?

3. Is there any good reason for not believing that all creatures might ultimately be redeemed?

19

Salvation in Feminist Perspective

There is a sense in which this section should not need to be included, in that all theology should be written embracing the insights of feminism. Unfortunately this is not yet the case, and the standard books on redemption miss it out entirely. My own set of stories will, I know, be criticized for embodying all sorts of implicit patriarchal assumptions, and it is obvious that, if a woman had written them, they would have looked different. (I thought of reversing Tom's and Rebecca's roles but could not make it stick.) 'Feminism', of course, is not all of a piece, as the speaker at the Dominican house recognized, but we can still ask what it is we learn from feminism about salvation which we do not learn from the rest of the tradition.

In her classic book *Sexism and God Talk* (SCM Press 1983), Rosemary Radford Ruether raises the question of whether a male saviour can save women. She does not write about redemption or atonement as such, but sees the need to get back beyond the patriarchalization of christology to the Jesus of the Synoptic Gospels, who, in his critique of religious and social hierarchy, has something to offer feminists. Jesus is the liberator, the representative of liberated humanity, announcing a new humanity through a non-hierarchical lifestyle. Redemption is not, on this account, 'once for all'. 'Christic personhood' continues in the church, and it is 'redemptive personhood' which goes ahead of us, calling us to further dimensions of human liberation. There are aspects here of exemplary ideas of atonement, of the continuation of redemption through the work of the Spirit, and of the idea of liberation from the powers, in this case, patriarchy.

Other feminist theologians have raised the question about sin. For male theologians from Augustine to Barth pride has always been the paradigm sin. In their hubris human beings reject God. But, feminist theologians have asked, is this really appropriate to women's experience? Is not the paradigm form of women's sin passivity, a failure to act, being too compliant? It is not just the raging male ego that is the problem, but a female self-effacing, self-negating ego. There can be, and is, debate about how passive women really are, but the point is well made. What would redemption look like answering this form of sin?

An obvious answer is affirmation and empowerment. According to Carol Gilligan, whom the speaker in the story cites, both are found in the different way women go about things, rooted in their different patterns of socialization. Mary Grey finds the heart of a feminist theology of redemption in restoring broken relationships. Of course that is implicit in the biblical language about reconciliation, but its full scope is clouded if reconciliation with God is given absolute priority over our reconciliation with our neighbour. What is the source of this reconciliation? She talks of harnessing the power we know in relationships, which she roots in the divine. The passion for right relation goes beyond purely personal relationships to the struggle for justice, but it always comes back to the particular, to those damaged relationships which skew the noblest liberation movements. Jesus himself instantiates a life of redeeming relationship, living 'deep in relationship with the creative source of that power, committed to the incarnating of this creative re-sourcing, which continually gave birth to the kingdom of God'.[1] This is yet another instance of the need to understand atonement through the work of the Spirit.

Some feminist theologians have rejected the traditional Western doctrine of the atonement as necrophilic, and this is an objection that Tom raises at one or two points. Is it any wonder that so much violence results from an obsessive preoccupation with death? Others, whilst sensitive to the depths and complexities of this tradition, suggest giving birth as an

---

[1] Mary Grey, *Redeeming the Dream*, SPCK 1989, p. 151.

appropriate feminine image for the work of God, which is creative and redemptive at the same time. Pain is involved in giving birth, but it is not the pain of violence, but rather a pain which gives birth to a new world. The image can appeal to those passages in Scripture which compare God's feelings to those of a woman in labour. This kind of thinking is far readier to talk of co-creation than male theology has been, which is usually fiercely insistent on God's absolute independence from, and priority to, creation.

Over the past thirty years many feminists argued that a male saviour could not indeed save women, and the way women were marginalized within the church underlined the point. But then we can ask, can anybody save anybody else? Are we not all our own saviours? In this situation other feminists, and in particular Angela West, have gone back to the New Testament and found that redemption comes from one who is fundamentally Other. Christ is both like us and yet radically different, 'like us in all things but sin'. They find in some ostensibly radical feminism the kind of domestication of God which is implicit in idolatry – making God in our own image. But as Isaiah insisted with such marvellous scorn, we cannot be saved by our own creations, our own theories, ideals, religions and religiosities. The scale of the outrage against humanity is so vast, says Angela West, that if we are not redeemed by the truly Other, then we are wholly lost. Given the fact that we are all created by the traditions of which we are apart, we have to recognize our debt to church and tradition, and live uncomfortably within it, not abandoning feminist insights, but not making them into a new and isolated system either.

Questions for discussion

1. How do you react to the question of whether a male saviour can save women?

2. Of the feminist theologies outlined, which do you find the most satisfying, and why?

3. Some (male!) theologians have suggested that women are more in tune with God's redeeming purposes than men. What do you think?

20

Salvation and the Cosmos

In his letter to the Christians in Rome Paul extends the idea of salvation to the whole of the cosmos. He writes:

> The creation waits with eager longing for the revealing of the children of God; for the creation was subjected to futility, not of its own will but by the will of the one who subjected it, in hope that the creation itself will be set free from its bondage to decay and will obtain the freedom of the glory of the children of God (Rom. 8.19–20).

At first sight this is a very odd idea. God the Creator subjected creation to futility. Why? Paul's answer is that God chose that the whole of creation would have to wait for humankind, and for their representative, and saviour, Jesus. In his resurrection he is the first fruits for everything that is. Paul is presupposing that human beings are so much part of creation, taken out of dust as they originally were, that it is *pars pro toto* – what happens to them is an anticipation of what is going to happen to everything else. This is an idea, which was developed by the early Greek Fathers, and has always been part of Orthodox theology. For them what we chiefly need to be saved from is death. Death, according to Paul, is 'the last enemy' which has to be overcome (I Cor. 15.26). He looks forward to a time when 'death is swallowed up in victory', just as the author of Revelation hopes for a time when 'death will be no more' (Rev. 21.4). We have already encountered that idea in looking at the crucified God, and what happens to the victims of the terror of history. 'God became man,' said Athanasius, 'so that we might become gods.' What he has in mind is participation in the divine nature. But because human beings are part of the rest of creation – gluons and quarks like everything else, we would say today – then that too is destined for 'deification'. Christ's incarnation is therefore the fundamental salvific act, God taking upon Godself the nature of created reality, in order finally to redeem it from bondage, in Paul's words.

In our story Stephen, the Methodist minister, is concerned with the salvation of creation, but his starting point is the ecological crisis. This has the same starting point: that humans are bound up with creation. But dominating practices, anti-life behaviour in relation to the non-human world, threatens the whole of creation. One of the speakers at the harvest supper asks whether we can really sin against creation. In the Genesis story it is the violence of human beings which prompts the Flood, and the ecological crisis is a matter of violence against the created order. That we are bound up with creation means that, when we think of the salvation of the cosmos, we are not suddenly abandoning all the ideas we have explored hitherto. On the contrary, human liberation and peace with and for nature go together. Isaiah already anticipated this in his famous vision that

> The wolf shall live with the lamb,
>   the leopard shall lie down with the kid,
> the calf and the lion and the fatling together,
>   and a little child shall lead them . . .
> The nursing child shall play over the hole of the asp,
>   and the weaned child shall put its hand on the adder's den.
> They will not hurt or destroy on all my holy mountain
>
> (Isa. 11.6–9).

Once again we come across the idea that salvation means the end of violence, this time extending across the chain of creation.

Everyone is familiar with the division between religion and politics. From the sixteenth century on there was an analogous division between 'subjective' (what concerns the person) and

104

'objective' (what concerns the world), and between religion and science. Religion was concerned with the soul, science with the material world. Sooner or later science would solve all our problems. Religion got pushed into the remaining 'gaps'. The ecological crisis has helped show up how false this way of thinking is. Today we are forced to appreciate the way in which we are bound up with the whole created order. We can sense the longing of creation as passionately as Paul. Like him we have to hope (his key word) for it. Paul's thinking at this point is eschatological: that is, looking towards the fulfilment of all things in the new creation, and it is based on the resurrection. The risen Christ is described as the 'first fruits', 'the first to rise from the dead' (Acts 26.23), 'the firstborn from the dead' (Col. 1.18). The resurrection is begun in Christ but is continued by the Spirit of life, and will be completed on the last day. In a sense this is true of all thinking about salvation. It is true, for example, of the hope for the victims which Rebecca cherished. It is true of our own lives, as we look for the realization of who we truly are through judgment, forgiveness, and re-creation. For resurrection cannot be the playback of our life video. I once had a severely handicapped student who said, 'If resurrection means I have this body, I don't want resurrection.' But he speaks for all of us, for we all have failings and experiences with which we do not want to live for ever. Resurrection is the promise of healing, reconciliation, and being finally made whole. Finally, as we have seen in this section, resurrection is the promise for all created reality.

Questions for discussion

1. What do you make of the Orthodox Church's language about deification?

2. How important is the resurrection of the body to Christian ideas of salvation?

3. If creation has been 'subjected to futility, what are the implications for our use and understanding of the non-human creation?

21

Pulling the Threads Together

A famous story tells how the Victorian New Testament scholar and Bishop of Durham, Brooke Foss Westcott, was once travelling on a train and found himself in a carriage with a Salvation Army officer, who asked him what he would have said if asked whether he was saved? The bishop paused a moment, and then answered with a gentle smile: 'I should have said, "Do you mean *sotheis* [saved once for all in the past], *sozomenos* [being saved in the present], or *sesosmenos* [having been saved in the past with a salvation which goes on into the future]?"'[1] As we have seen in the stories and the explorations of the second part, salvation is as many textured as life, and resists all attempts to pin it down in neat schemes. I tried, for this book, to draw up a chart showing the correlation between those things we need to be saved from and what Christians believe about Christ's life and work. It ended up in a hopeless muddle because the interconnections were so dense. God engages with the whole of life, and schematization is bound to falsify this. However, by way of pulling threads together let us look briefly once more at those things from which we need to be saved.

First, there is 'sin', but this is a protean word. There are the seven deadlies, there is selfishness, there is the destruction and diminishment of life, there is what Karl Barth called 'the Lie', unaccountably missed out of the mediaeval list, there is alienation. In theological language the opposite of sin is 'grace'. Sin is opposition to God's free, joyful, life-giving, loving self-giving. It negates all those attributes.

When we are healthy, sin engenders guilt, just as a virus gives us a fever. A sense of guilt is a sign that we are not

---

[1]   Joseph Clayton, *Bishop Westcott*, in series *Leaders of the Church 1800–1900*, ed. G. W. E. Russell, Mowbray 1906, p. 111.

'hardened' but it can also be pathological, something from which we need deliverance. Persistence in sin can lead to the feeling, or the state, of being 'godforsaken' – that is, of complete exclusion of God from our life, and an option for everything which is anti-God.

Part of sin, but often not identified with it, is ignorance or stupidity. This is nothing to do with having poor GCSEs or not being able to do crosswords (at least, I hope it isn't, because I can't). It means rather a wilful blindness to the good and the true, a refusal to see what is right. We sometimes use the word 'ignorant' in this way in English. It is close to what Jesus means by the 'sin against the Holy Spirit', which was the insistence on calling what was patently good (the restoration of someone to health), evil.

In the Lord's Prayer Jesus teaches us to pray, 'Deliver us from evil'. Evil, I have argued, represents a dimension which is bigger than personal sin. Sin is part of it, but not the whole of it. It represents those threats which dwarf us – the threat to the environment, the threat of nuclear war, the power of the market, which Jesus called Mammon. Every age has its own versions of the powers which hold us in thrall, and from which we need deliverance.

Finally, there is the dimension of suffering in all its manifold forms. Jesus himself showed quite clearly in his ministry that ill health, death, and by implication all the other things which oppress us as embodied creatures, are things from which we need 'saving'. These things may have no relation to sin at all. Think of the loss of a child through meningitis. On the other hand, they may be related to sin in the closest possible way, as our El Salvador and Holocaust stories illustrate.

Readers will, I hope, want to add to this their own examples of that from which we need to be saved. Is there salvation from these ills? Not everyone thinks so. Many of our contemporaries are convinced that we are on our own, and that belief in salvation manifests a puerile sense of dependence. If I do not agree, it is at least partly because I believe dependence is part of the fullness of our humanity and that it does not detract from it at all.

Others seek salvation in self-help, psychotherapy of one kind or another, transcendental meditation, 'centring'. On the whole they understand salvation in terms of maturity. There is no reason to despise such therapies, but there is a question as to how far they take us. The same question attends political accounts of salvation. In particular, death is always an unanswered problem.

Christians find salvation in Christ, but if we are to understand that in its fullness it is vital to attend to the whole biblical record. The Gospels are not, as they were famously described at the end of the nineteenth century, 'passion stories with long introductions'. We learn about salvation from every part of the gospel story, and from the whole of Scripture.

Healing, release from oppression, the provision of basic human amenities such as schooling, health care, sewage, and so forth are, I have argued, obvious extensions of Jesus' healing ministry. In the same way the dimension of salvation I have explored in the chapter 'Example' is a continuation of Jesus' immensely important teaching ministry. From Jesus' resurrection flows our victory over death, and for St Paul, as we saw, the salvation of the whole cosmos from 'futility'. All of this stands in relation to Christ's death, traditionally the focus of all Christian reflection on salvation. *Ave crux, unica spes*!: 'Hail, O Cross, our only hope!', sang our mediaeval ancestors. I have tried to explore some of the ways in which this has been understood: as 'paying the price for sin', as a sacrifice for sin, as Jesus bearing our sin away as a scapegoat, as identification with the victim. I will not repeat here the various questions I have raised in relation to these ideas. What I will emphasize, once again, is that none of these ideas make sense without Pentecost. Past event – what happened on Calvary – becomes present salvation in our lives and in our society through the ongoing work of God as Spirit, seeking us out, meeting sin with grace and forgiveness, outflanking evil, healing our wounds and, most importantly, going ahead of us. In the stories in Acts Peter and Philip both discovered that God the Spirit was ahead of them in the household of a Roman centurion or an Ethiopian eunuch. Salvation had gone ahead of the church. Too often the church has wanted to assert control of the process, but God, the One who loves in freedom, cannot thus be tamed. God invites us constantly to learn anew the dimensions, the 'deepest freshness deep down things', to use Gerald Manley Hopkins' phrase, of salvation. It is a gracious invitation to which God wants us to respond.

Further Reading

There are a huge number of books available on the theme of atonement, many of them standard run-throughs of the main arguments. A good place to start with is novels:

Dostoevsky's *The Brothers Karamazov* is indispensable.

Graham Greene raises many issues related to redemption in *The Heart of the Matter,* and *The Power and the Glory.*

Doris Lessing's five-novel sequence *The Children of Violence* does the same.

George Eliot's *Middlemarch* ends with ongoing redemption and explores the theme at many levels.

Elie Wiesel's *Night* (Penguin 1981) is an autobiographical account of his time in Auschwitz, and seminal for much contemporary reflection on redemption.

Amongst theological works some of the most important are:

L & C. Boff, *Salvation and Liberation* (Orbis Books 1988).

Explores the relation and distinction between the two ideas.

Charles Elliott, *Memory and Salvation* (Darton, Longman & Todd 1995).

A study of the contribution of psychoanalysis to our understanding of atonement.

Paul Fiddes, *Past Event and Present Salvation* (Darton, Longman & Todd 1989).

A useful survey of atonement doctrine.

R. Girard, *Things Hidden From the Foundation of the World* (Athlone Press 1987).

Brilliant and important, but also tendentious.

T. J. Gorringe, *God's Just Vengeance* (CUP 1996).

A reflection on the mutual interaction of atonement and criminal justice.

T. J. Gorringe, *Redeeming Time* (Darton, Longman & Todd 1986).

An attempt to reflect on the atonement through Freire's *Pedagogy of the Oppressed* (Penguin 1972).

Mary Grey, *Redeeming the Dream* (SPCK 1989).

A sympathetic and imaginative account of redemption from a feminist perspective, drawing widely on Western literature.

G. Gutiérrez, *A Theology of Liberation* (SCM Press 1972, 2nd edn 1988).

The classic text of liberation theology, and a cogent presentation of liberation as salvation.

R. C. Moberly, *Atonement and Personality* (John Murray 1901).

Still the greatest Anglican contribution to the theology of the atonement.

Jürgen Moltmann, *The Crucified God* (SCM Press 1974).

A modern classic. The sixth chapter, which is the heart of the book, is dense and difficult, but repays repeated reading.

Jürgen Moltmann, *God in Creation* (SCM Press 1985) and *The Coming of God* (SCM Press 1996).

Both explore the idea of the salvation of the cosmos.

R. Schwager, *Must there be Scapegoats?* (Harper & Row, San Francisco 1987).

An exploration of the violence bound up with Christian atonement theology, and of alternatives.

Angela West, *Deadly Innocence* (Mowbray 1995).

An account of modern feminism from a theological perspective, which puts searching questions from the standpoint of redemption.

Walter Wink, *Naming the Powers* (1984), *Unmasking the Powers* (1986), *Engaging the Powers* (1992). All Fortress Press.

These books are a profound study of systems of domination, and the way in which Christ liberates us from them, a form of biblical theology enriched by sociological and psycho-therapeutic insight.